INTERFUEL
SUBSTITUTION

INTERFUEL SUBSTITUTION

Apostolos Serletis
University of Calgary, Canada

 **World Scientific**

NEW JERSEY · LONDON · SINGAPORE · BEIJING · SHANGHAI · HONG KONG · TAIPEI · CHENNAI

Published by

World Scientific Publishing Co. Pte. Ltd.

5 Toh Tuck Link, Singapore 596224

USA office: 27 Warren Street, Suite 401-402, Hackensack, NJ 07601

UK office: 57 Shelton Street, Covent Garden, London WC2H 9HE

British Library Cataloguing-in-Publication Data
A catalogue record for this book is available from the British Library.

INTERFUEL SUBSTITUTION

ISBN-13 978-981-4374-36-1
ISBN-10 981-4374-36-9

In-house Editor: Samantha Yong

Printed in Singapore.

Contents

Preface

The effects of output growth and changing fuel prices on the demand for energy depend on interfuel substitution and the substitutability of energy and other factors of production. Over the years, these issues have attracted a great deal of attention in a large number of energy demand studies, with most of these studies taking the approach of using a flexible functional form for the underlying aggregator function, following Diewert's (1971) influential paper. In fact, this approach to empirical energy demand analysis was pioneered by Berndt and Wood (1975), Fuss (1977), and Pindyck (1979). It involves specifying a differentiable form for the cost function, and applying Shephard's lemma to derive the resulting cost share (or input-output) equations. Using these equations and relevant data, one then could estimate the parameters and produce inferences about the demand for fuels (including those about the own- and cross-price elasticities as well as the elasticities of substitution).

Although the role of energy in the structure of production has been the focus of a large number of econometric studies, the evidence on interfactor and interfuel substitutability is mixed. For example, the early studies by Berndt and Wood (1975), Fuss (1977) and Magnus (1979) all used time series data for a single country and found substitutability between energy and labor, but complementarity between energy and capital. Also, Fuss (1977), using Canadian data, found oil, gas, and coal to be substitutes, but found no substitutability between each of these energy inputs and electricity. Moreover, Pindyck (1979), taking a similar approach to that used by Fuss (1977), used pooled time-series data for a cross section of countries and found energy and labor to be substitutes and also energy and capital to be substitutes, and not complements as earlier studies had indicated. Such variability in results can be partly explained by significant inherent differences between short- and long-run adjustments.

In this book I am not interested in interfactor substitution. Instead, I am interested in interfuel substitution, an issue that is (and will likely remain) an important topic of inquiry for many years, as governments around the world seek to set policies that are intended to restrain carbon emissions or steer economies toward or away from certain fuels. In this regard, it should be noted that the results of most energy and climate change policy models, no matter whether they are partial equilibrium or general equilibrium type, are highly sensitive to elasticity parameters, particularly the elasticities of interfuel substitution. However, there exists only limited recent literature estimating such elasticity parameters. Moreover, with the exception of a few sporadic local articles, there is still a huge void in the literature dealing with energy demand and interfuel substitution in developing countries. This book contributes to filling the literature gap by estimating interfuel substitution elasticities through the use of recent advances in microeconometrics and the use of recent international data for a number of OECD and non-OECD countries.

Over the years, there has been a large number of studies investigating interfuel substitution and the demand for energy — see, for example, Uri (1979), Considine (1989), Hall (1986) and Jones (1995), among others. The major contributions in this area, however, are quite outdated by now, since their data incorporate observations before the 1970s. Also, very few studies deal with energy demand and interfuel substitution in developing countries, probably due to the lack of reliable data at that time. Moreover, most of this literature ignores the theoretical regularity conditions of neoclassical microeconomic theory. However, as Barnett (2002, p. 199) put it, without satisfying the theoretical regularity conditions,

"the second-order conditions for optimizing behavior fail, and duality theory fails. The resulting first-order conditions, demand functions, and supply functions become invalid."

In this book, I investigate short- and long-run interfuel (i.e., oil, natural gas, coal, and electricity) substitution, using international time series data. In doing so, I investigate interfuel substitution within the industrial, residential, transportation and electricity generation sectors, since the structure of interfuel substitution is different for different sectors of use. My objective is to improve our understanding of how economic growth, government policies, and the development and implementation of new technologies, will affect interfuel substitution and the demand for energy in the future. In order to achieve this, I use recent advances in microeconometrics, including duality theory and flexible functional forms and provide inference, and also a policy perspective, using parameter estimates that are consistent with the theoretical regularity conditions of neoclassical microeconomic theory.

Because the existing major contributions in this area are quite outdated, since their data incorporate few (if any) observations subsequent to the oil price shocks in the 1970s, I use the most recent data (since 1980), published by the International Energy Agency (IEA), for a number of OECD and non-OECD countries (including China and India) for which reliable data are available. This is important as recent IEA projections show that non-OECD countries will account for close to 90% of the increase in energy demand in the next 20 years, with China and India likely to account for over 50% of this growth. In particular, I provide evidence for six high-income countries (Canada, France, Japan, Italy, the United Kingdom and the United States), for five upper-middle to high-income economies (Poland, Hungary, Mexico, Turkey and Venezuela), and for four lower-middle to low-income economies (China, India, South Africa and Thailand).

Of the four essays which follow, Chapter 1 is new, while Chapters 2, 3, and 4 are reprints, with relatively minor revisions, of recently published work. The revisions which I have made were meant to eliminate repetitive passages and a certain amount of overlap among the individual essays.

A number of institutions and individuals have made the completion of these essays possible. The World Bank Research Support Program provided financial support for the essays that appear in Chapters 3 and 4 of this book. However, the views expressed in this book do not necessarily represent the World Bank and its affiliated organizations. I would like to thank my coauthors, Govinda Timilsina and Olexandr Vasetsky, of the original papers that have been reprinted in this book as Chapters 2, 3, and 4. Thanks are also due to the colleagues that commented on one or more of these essays, William Barnett, Erwin Diewert, Shahidur R. Khandker, Guohua Feng, Daniel Gordon, Alexander David, the Editor of *The Energy Journal*, James Smith, the Editors of *Energy Economics*, Beng Ang, Richard Tol, and John Weyant, and the anonymous referees of *The Energy Journal* and *Energy Economics*. Of course, none of them is responsible for the finished product.

Finally, I would like to thank Joanne Canape for a thoroughly professional job of preparing the camera-ready copy of this book. This work would not have been possible without her help.

Chapter 1

Empirical Energy Demand Analysis

1.1 Introduction

In this chapter I discuss the econometric approach to estimation of theory-based models of the demand for energy and interfuel substitution. Although the empirical estimation of production functions began with Cobb and Douglas (1928), the estimation of a flexible production function, or its dual, a cost function, or the convex conjugate of the two, a profit function, began with Diewert's (1971) influential paper and the introduction of the generalized Leontief flexible functional form. I thus present an overview of techniques for theory based econometric analysis, including price elasticities and elasticities of substitution.

I also present a discussion of two well-known flexible functional forms — the locally flexible generalized Leontief of Diewert (1971) and the translog of Christensen *et al.* (1975). I argue that flexible functional forms have given researchers the ability to model consumer and producer behavior with no local restrictions on the nature of the substitutability/complementarity relationship between pairs of goods. Unfortunately, however, theoretical regularity restrictions met by simpler forms, such as the Cobb-Douglas and the constant elasticity of substitution, or by globally regular flexible functional forms, might not be satisfied with most locally-flexible functional forms.

I thus pay explicit attention to the theoretical regularity conditions of positivity, monotonicity, and curvature and argue that much of the older literature on the demand for energy and interfuel substitution ignores economic regularity. I argue that unless economic regularity is attained by luck, flexible functional forms should always be estimated subject to regularity, as suggested by Barnett (2002) and Barnett and Pasupathy (2003).

1.2   The Econometric Approach

The econometric approach to the demand for energy and interfuel substitution involves estimating the parameters of an aggregator function, production or cost function. Let's start by assuming a production function

$$y = f(\boldsymbol{x}, t) \tag{1.1}$$

where y is output, f is a continuous twice differentiable nondecreasing and quasiconcave function of a vector of inputs $\boldsymbol{x} \geq \boldsymbol{0}$, and t denotes a technology index, so that technical change can also be defined as $\partial f(\boldsymbol{x}, t) / \partial t$.

Under the assumption that firms competitively minimize the cost of production subject to producing a given amount of output, then the technology (1.1) is completely described by the dual cost function

$$C = C(\boldsymbol{p}, y, t) = yc(\boldsymbol{p}, t) \tag{1.2}$$

with the second equality assuming constant returns to scale. In equation (1.2), C is a nondecreasing, linearly homogeneous and concave function of prices, $\boldsymbol{p} > \boldsymbol{0}$, and c is the corresponding unit cost function — for a review of duality theory, see Diewert (1974).

To obtain equations that are amenable to estimation, I apply Shephard's lemma to equation (1.2) to get

$$x_i = \frac{\partial C(\boldsymbol{p}, y, t)}{\partial p_i}, \qquad i = 1, \cdots, n \tag{1.3}$$

or a more convenient equation for estimation purposes, by dividing through by y,

$$\frac{x_i}{y} = \frac{1}{y} \frac{\partial C(\boldsymbol{p}, y, t)}{\partial p_i}, \qquad i = 1, \cdots, n.$$

Factor substitution is calculated, using both Allen and Morishima elasticities of substitution. The Allen-Uzawa elasticity of substitution between inputs i and j is given by

$$\sigma_{ij}^a(\boldsymbol{p}, y, t) = \frac{C(\boldsymbol{p}, y, t) C_{ij}(\boldsymbol{p}, y, t)}{C_i(\boldsymbol{p}, y, t) C_j(\boldsymbol{p}, y, t)}$$

where the i, j subscripts refer to the first and second partial derivatives of $C(\boldsymbol{p}, y, t)$ with respect to input prices p_i and p_j. The Morishima elasticity of substitution between inputs i and j is given by

$$\sigma_{ij}^m(\boldsymbol{p}, y, t) = \frac{p_j C_{ij}(\boldsymbol{p}, y, t)}{C_i(\boldsymbol{p}, y, t)} - \frac{p_j C_{jj}(\boldsymbol{p}, y, t)}{C_j(\boldsymbol{p}, y, t)}.$$

If $\sigma_{ij}^a > 0$ (that is, if increasing the jth price increases the optimal quantity of input i), we say that inputs i and j are Allen-Uzawa (net) substitutes. If $\sigma_{ij}^a < 0$, they are Allen-Uzawa (net) complements. Similarly, if $\sigma_{ij}^m > 0$ (that is, if increasing the jth price increases the optimal quantity of input i relative to the optimal quantity of input j), we say that input j is a Morishima (net) substitute for input i. If $\sigma_{ij}^m < 0$, input j is a Morishima net complement to input i. The Allen elasticities provide immediate qualitative comparative-static information about the effect of price changes on absolute input shares, whereas the Morishima elasticities immediately yield both qualitative and quantitative information about the effect of price changes on relative input shares.

The familiar price elasticities

$$\eta_{ij} = \frac{\partial x_i \left(\boldsymbol{p}, y, t \right)}{\partial p_j} \frac{p_j}{x_i \left(\boldsymbol{p}, y, t \right)}$$

could also be calculated as

$$\eta_{ij} = s_j \sigma_{ij}^a$$

where s_j is the cost share of input j in total production costs. Notice that the price elasticities must satisfy the following condition

$$\sum_{j=1}^n \eta_{ij} = 0, \qquad i = 1, \cdots, n.$$

1.3 Theoretical Regularity

As required by neoclassical microeconomic theory, the cost function has to satisfy the following properties:

  i) homogeneity
  ii) positivity
  iii) monotonicity, and
  iv) curvature.

Homogeneity requires that the cost function be linearly homogeneous in input prices. Positivity requires that the estimated cost be positive for all the data observations. Monotonicity requires that the first-order derivatives of the cost function, $\partial C \left(\boldsymbol{p}, y, t \right) / \partial p_i$ $(i = 1, \cdots, n)$, which correspond to input demands, be nonnegative. Curvature requires that the cost function, $C \left(\boldsymbol{p}, y, t \right)$, be a concave function of prices or, equivalently, that the Hessian matrix of the cost function be negative semidefinite.

Together, properties (ii)-(iv) are called the *regularity conditions*. In the terminology of Caves and Christensen (1980), a cost function is *regular*, if it satisfies the above properties. Similarly, the *regular region* is the set of prices at which a cost function satisfies the regularity conditions. Clearly, regularity should not be treated as being equivalent to curvature alone; instead it includes all the three above conditions, namely, positivity, monotonicity, and curvature.

1.4   Flexible Functional Forms

By substituting different unit cost functions into (1.2), we can get different total cost functions. For many years, econometricians used *globally regular* functional forms, such as the Cobb-Douglas and the Constant Elasticity of Substitution (CES) forms, to approximate the generating functions of neoclassical microeconomic theory such as the unit cost function in (1.2). However, as noted by Uzawa (1964), although globally regular forms satisfy everywhere the theoretical regularity conditions, they do not provide the capability to attain arbitrary elasticities of substitution.

In recent years, most empirical studies make use of duality theory and the *flexible* functional forms method to approximate aggregator functions, following Diewert's (1971) influential paper and the introduction of the generalized Leontief flexible production function. A flexible functional form is an approximation to an arbitrary function, with parameters that can be chosen to make the value of the first and second derivatives of the approximation equal to the first and second derivatives of the true function at any point — see Diewert (1973) for more details.

In what follows, I briefly discuss two widely used locally flexible cost functional forms [following closely Feng and Serletis (2008)] — the generalized Leontief and the basic translog. Of course, there are many other possibilities, but I selected these functional forms because they provide a representation of the locally flexible functional forms that are in the widest use in applied work.

I also pay explicit attention to theoretical regularity, since the usefulness of flexible functional forms depends on whether they satisfy the regularity conditions of positivity, monotonicity, and curvature. In fact, in the literature there has been a tendency to ignore regularity and as Barnett (2002, p. 199) put it in his *Journal of Econometrics* Fellow's opinion article, without satisfaction of all three theoretical regularity conditions

"the second-order conditions for optimizing behavior fail, and
duality theory fails. The resulting first-order conditions, demand functions, and supply functions become invalid."

1.4.1 *The Generalized Leontief*

By substituting the generalized Leontief (GL) unit cost function [see Diewert (1971)] into (1.2), we get the GL specification

$$C\left(\boldsymbol{p}, y, t\right) = y \left(\sum_{i=1}^{n} \sum_{j=1}^{n} \beta_{ij} p_i^{1/2} p_j^{1/2} + \sum_{i=1}^{n} \beta_{it} p_i t \right) \qquad (1.4)$$

where $\beta_{ij} = \beta_{ji}$. Using Shephard's lemma, and dividing through by y,
yields optimal input-output demand equations, as follows

$$\frac{x_i}{y} = \sum_{j=1}^{n} \beta_{ij} p_j^{1/2} p_i^{-1/2} + \beta_{it} t, \qquad i = 1, \cdots, n. \qquad (1.5)$$

Notice that all the parameters of the GL cost function (1.4) can be obtained
by estimating only (1.5). It is to be noted that when $i = j$ in (1.5),
$p_j^{1/2} p_i^{-1/2} = 1$ and so β_{ii} is a constant term in the ith input-output equation.
When $\beta_{ij} = 0$ for all i, j, $i \neq j$, then input-output demand equations are
independent of relative prices and the cross-price elasticities are zero.

Caves and Christensen (1980) have shown that the GL has satisfactory
local properties when technology is nearly homothetic and substitution is
low. However, when technology is not homothetic and substitution increases, they show that the GL has a rather small regularity region.

Concavity of the cost function (1.4) requires that the Hessian matrix
is negative semidefinite. We can therefore impose local concavity (that
is, at the reference point) by evaluating the Hessian terms of (1.4) at the
reference point, where all prices and output are unity, as follows

$$\boldsymbol{H}_{ij} = -\delta_{ij} \left(\sum_{j=1, j \neq i}^{n} \beta_{ij}/2 \right) + (1 - \delta_{ij}) \beta_{ij}/2$$

where $\delta_{ij} = 1$ if $i = j$ and 0 otherwise. By replacing $\boldsymbol{H}$ by $-1/2\ \boldsymbol{KK'}$,
where $\boldsymbol{K}$ is an $n \times n$ lower triangular matrix and $\boldsymbol{K'}$ its transpose, the
above can be written as

$$-\frac{1}{2} \left(\boldsymbol{KK'} \right)_{ij} = -\delta_{ij} \left(\sum_{j=1, j \neq i}^{n} \beta_{ij}/2 \right) + (1 - \delta_{ij}) \beta_{ij}/2. \qquad (1.6)$$

There are two things that should be noted here. First, the β_{ii} $(i = 1, \cdots, n)$ do not appear in (1.6), thus leaving β_{ii} $(i = 1, \cdots, n)$ unrestricted. Second, the fact that the elements in the same row of $\boldsymbol{H}$ add to zero, that is

$$\sum_{j=1}^{n} \boldsymbol{H}_{ij} = - \left(\sum_{j=1, j \neq i}^{n} \beta_{ij}/2 \right) + \sum_{j=1, j \neq i}^{n} \beta_{ij}/2 = 0, \qquad i = 1, \cdots, n$$

implies the following restrictions on $\boldsymbol{K}$

$$\sum_{i=1}^{n} k_{ij} = 0, \qquad j = 1, \cdots, n \tag{1.7}$$

i.e. the elements in the same column of $\boldsymbol{K}$ add to zero, where the k_{ij} terms are the elements of the replacement matrix $\boldsymbol{K}$. (1.7) can be easily shown by expanding out (1.6). Obtaining the main diagonal elements of $\boldsymbol{K}$, k_{ii}, expressed in terms of k_{ij} $(i \neq j)$ and then substituting them into (1.6), we will obtain β_{ij} $(1 \leq i < j \leq n)$ which are expressed only in terms of k_{ij} $(1 \leq j < i \leq n)$.

As an example, for the case of three inputs $(n = 3)$, we can use the restrictions (1.7) and the lower triangular structure of $\boldsymbol{K}$ in order to eliminate the diagonal elements of $\boldsymbol{K}$, k_{ii} $(i = 1, 2, 3)$, as follows

$$k_{11} = -k_{21} - k_{31}$$
$$k_{22} = -k_{32}$$
$$k_{33} = 0.$$

Substituting the above restrictions in (1.6), we obtain

$$\beta_{12} = -k_{21}k_{11} = k_{21}(k_{21} + k_{31})$$
$$\beta_{13} = -k_{31}k_{11} = k_{31}(k_{21} + k_{31})$$
$$\beta_{23} = -(k_{21}k_{31} + k_{22}k_{32}) = -k_{21}k_{31} + k_{32}^2$$

which guarantees concavity of the cost function at the reference point and may also induce concavity of the cost function at other data points. As already noted above, β_{11}, β_{22}, and β_{33} in this example are unrestricted and do not have to be expressed in terms of the elements of $\boldsymbol{K}$. Also, the flexibility of the GL is not destroyed because the $n(n-1)/2$ elements of $\boldsymbol{K}$ just replace the $n(n-1)/2$ elements of $\boldsymbol{H}$ in the estimation.

1.4.2 The Translog

The translog specification, due to Christensen *et al.* (1975), is obtained by substituting the translog unit cost function into (1.2) to get

$$\ln C\left(\boldsymbol{p}, y, t\right) = \ln y + \beta_0 + \beta_t t + \sum_{i=1}^{n} \beta_i \ln p_i$$

$$+ \frac{1}{2} \sum_{i=1}^{n} \sum_{j=1}^{n} \beta_{ij} \ln p_i \ln p_j + \sum_{i=1}^{n} \beta_{it} t \ln p_i + \frac{1}{2} \beta_{tt} t^2 \qquad (1.8)$$

where $\beta_{ij} = \beta_{ji}$. Homogeneity of degree one in prices (given y) implies the following restrictions

$$\sum_{i=1}^{n} \beta_i = 1, \quad \sum_{i=1}^{n} \beta_{ij} = \sum_{j=1}^{n} \beta_{ji} = \sum_{i=1}^{n} \beta_{it} = 0. \qquad (1.9)$$

Although we could estimate (1.8) directly, efficiency gains can be realized by estimating the optimal cost-minimizing input demand equations, transformed into cost-share equations, as follows

$$s_i = \frac{p_i x_i}{C} = \beta_i + \sum_{j=1}^{n} \beta_{ij} \ln p_j + \beta_{it} t \qquad (1.10)$$

where $\sum_{i=1}^{n} p_i x_i = C$.

Guilkey *et al.* (1983) show that the translog is globally regular if and only if technology is Cobb-Douglas. In other words, the translog performs well if substitution between all factors is close to unity. They also show that the regularity properties of the translog model deteriorate rapidly when substitution diverges from unity.

The Hessian matrix of the translog cost function at the reference point, where all prices and output are set to one, will be negative semidefinite if the following matrix is negative semidefinite

$$\boldsymbol{H}_{ij} = \beta_{ij} + \beta_i \beta_j - \delta_{ij} \beta_i, \qquad i, j = 1, \cdots, n$$

with $\delta_{ij} = 1$ if $i = j$ and 0 otherwise. Local concavity can be imposed at the reference point as in Ryan and Wales (2000) by setting $\boldsymbol{H} = -\boldsymbol{K}\boldsymbol{K}'$, as follows

$$\beta_{ij} + \beta_i \beta_j - \delta_{ij} \beta_i = \left(-\boldsymbol{K}\boldsymbol{K}'\right)_{ij}, \qquad i, j = 1, \cdots, n \qquad (1.11)$$

where (as before) $\boldsymbol{K}$ is a lower triangular matrix. Noting that $\sum_{j=1}^{n} \beta_{ij} = 0$ and $\sum_{j=1}^{n} \beta_j = 0$ (see equation (1.9)), it can be easily shown that

$$\sum_{j=1}^{n} \boldsymbol{H}_{ij} = \sum_{j=1}^{n} \left(\beta_{ij} - \beta_i \delta_{ij} + \beta_i \beta_j\right) = 0 \qquad (1.12)$$

i.e. the elements in the same row of H add to zero. Further, (1.12) implies the following restriction on the elements of K

$$\sum_{i=1}^{n} k_{ij} = 0, \qquad j = 1, \cdots, n \qquad (1.13)$$

i.e., the elements in the same column of K add to zero. Again, (1.13) can be shown by expanding out $H = -KK'$, where H satisfies (1.12). Combining (1.11) and (1.13), we can replace the elements of $B = [\beta_{ij}]$ by those of K. It should be noted that, unlike in the case of the generalized Leontief, β_{ii} $(i = 1, \cdots, n)$ are restricted in this case.

For the case with three inputs $(n = 3)$, equations (1.11) and (1.13) imply the following restrictions on the elements of K

$$\beta_{11} = -k_{11}^2 + \beta_1 - \beta_1^2 = -(k_{21} + k_{31})^2 + \beta_1 - \beta_1^2$$

$$\beta_{12} = -k_{11}k_{21} - \beta_1\beta_2 = (k_{21} + k_{31})k_{21} - \beta_1\beta_2$$

$$\beta_{13} = -k_{11}k_{31} - \beta_1\beta_3 = (k_{21} + k_{31})k_{31} - \beta_1\beta_3$$

$$\beta_{22} = -(k_{21}^2 + k_{22}^2) + \beta_2 - \beta_2^2 = -k_{21}^2 - k_{32}^2 + \beta_2 - \beta_2^2$$

$$\beta_{23} = -(k_{21}k_{31} + k_{22}k_{32}) - \beta_2\beta_3 = -k_{21}k_{31} + k_{32}^2 - \beta_2\beta_3$$

$$\beta_{33} = -(k_{31}^2 + k_{32}^2 + k_{33}^2) + \beta_3 - \beta_3^2 = -(k_{31}^2 + k_{32}^2) + \beta_3 - \beta_3^2$$

which guarantee concavity of the cost function at the reference point and may also induce concavity of the cost function at other data points. Again, the flexibility of the translog specification is not destroyed because the $n(n-1)/2$ elements of K just replace the $n(n-1)/2$ elements of B in the estimation.

1.5   Estimation Issues

In order to estimate equation systems such as (1.5) and (1.10), a stochastic component, ϵ_t, is added to the set of input-output equations or share equations as follows

$$\boldsymbol{w}_t = \boldsymbol{\psi}\left(\boldsymbol{p}_t, y, t, \boldsymbol{\theta}\right) + \boldsymbol{\epsilon}_t, \qquad (1.14)$$

where $\boldsymbol{w} = (w_1, \cdots, w_n)'$ is the vector of input-output ratios in the case of the GL model and that of input shares in the case of the translog model. $\boldsymbol{\epsilon}_t$ is a vector of stochastic errors and we assume that $\boldsymbol{\epsilon} \sim N\left(\boldsymbol{0}, \boldsymbol{\Omega}\right)$ where $\boldsymbol{0}$ is a null vector and $\boldsymbol{\Omega}$ is the $n \times n$ symmetric positive definite error covariance matrix. Also,

$$\psi\left(\boldsymbol{p}_t, y, t, \boldsymbol{\theta}\right) = \left(\psi_1\left(\boldsymbol{p}_t, y, t, \boldsymbol{\theta}\right), \cdots, \psi_n\left(\boldsymbol{p}_t, y, t, \boldsymbol{\theta}\right)\right)'$$

and $\psi_i\left(\boldsymbol{p}_t, y, t, \boldsymbol{\theta}\right)$ is given by the right-hand side of each of (1.5) and (1.10).

In the case of the translog model, since the shares in (1.10) sum to unity, the random disturbances corresponding to the share equations sum to zero and this yields a singular covariance matrix of errors. Barten (1969) has shown that full information maximum likelihood estimates of the parameters can be obtained by arbitrarily deleting any one equation. The resulting estimates are invariant with respect to the equation deleted and the parameter estimates of the deleted equation can be recovered from the restrictions imposed.

Another issue concerning the stochastic specification is that of endogeneity. At the individual firm level, it may be reasonably assumed that input prices on the right hand side of (1.14) are exogenous. At the more aggregated level, however, input prices are less likely to be exogenous. In the literature, the possibility of endogeneity has been addressed by using iterative three-stage least squares (3SLS), but the results generally have been about the same as those with iterative Zellner estimation — see, for example, Barnett *et al.* (1991). Diewert and Fox (2008) also argue that instrumental variables estimation may be more biased, since the instruments may not be completely exogenous, and Burnside (1996) shows that results can vary markedly depending on the set of instruments used.

Finally, the theoretical regularity conditions can be checked as follows:

- Positivity can be checked by checking if the estimated cost is positive,
$$C\left(\boldsymbol{p}, y, t\right) > 0.$$

- Monotonicity can be checked by direct computation of the values of the first gradient vector of the estimated cost function with respect to $\boldsymbol{p}$. It is satisfied if
$$\nabla_{\boldsymbol{p}} C\left(\boldsymbol{p}, y, t\right) > 0.$$

- Curvature requires the Hessian matrix of the cost function to be negative semidefinite and can be checked by performing a Cholesky factorization of that matrix and checking whether the Cholesky values are nonpositive [since a matrix is negative semidefinite if its Cholesky factors are nonpositive — see Lau (1978, Theorem 3.2)]. Curvature can also be checked by examining the eigenvalues of the Hessian matrix provided that the monotonicity condition holds. It requires that these eigenvalues be negative or zero.

1.6   Concluding Comments

I have provided a theoretical discussion of the demand systems approach to the demand for energy and interfuel substitution. I also discussed two locally flexible functional forms. Of course, as I will mention later in this book, there are many other possibilities, but I selected these functional forms in this chapter, because they provide a representation of the locally flexible functional forms that are in the widest use in applied work. I also want to emphasize that it would be preferable if one could nest at least some flexible functional forms, so that the choice between them could be the subject of a statistical hypothesis test. This is currently possible for those flexible functional forms that have interpretations as Taylor series expansions. In general, however, given known estimation techniques, it is not possible to nest flexible functional forms with different approximation properties.

Chapter 2

Interfuel Substitution in the United States*

2.1 Introduction

In this chapter, we use the locally flexible translog functional form to investigate the demand for energy and interfuel substitution in the United States. In doing so, however, we use recent advances in microeconometrics in an attempt to produce inference consistent with theoretical regularity. In particular, motivated by the widespread practice of ignoring theoretical regularity, we estimate the model subject to the theoretical regularity conditions of neoclassical microeconomic theory, using methods developed by Diewert and Wales (1987) and Ryan and Wales (2000).

Because the existing major contributions in this area are quite outdated, since their data incorporate few (if any) observations subsequent to the oil price shocks in the 1970s, we use the most recent data, published by the U.S. Energy Information Administration (EIA). Moreover, in addition to investigating interfuel substitution possibilities in total energy demand in the United States, we also examine interfuel substitution possibilities in energy demand by sector (industrial sector, commercial sector, residential sector, and electricity-generation sector). Finally, we test for weak separability, using a flexible functional form interpretation of the translog functional form, with the objective of discovering the structure of the functional form in total U.S. energy demand as well as energy demand by sector.

The rest of the chapter is organized as follows. Section 2.2 briefly sketches the neoclassical energy problem. Section 2.3 discusses estimation issues while Section 2.4 discusses the data and Section 2.5 presents and

---

*This article was published in *Energy Economics*, Vol 32, Serletis, Apostolos, Govinda Timilsina, and Olexandr Vasetsky, "Interfuel Substitution in the United States," 737-745. Copyright Elsevier (2010).

assesses the results in terms of their consistency with optimizing behavior and explores the economic significance of the results. The final section concludes.

2.2   Theoretical Foundations

As in Fuss (1977), we take the econometric approach, assuming a production function of the form

$$Y = f(E, L, M, K, t) \qquad (2.1)$$

where Y is a gross output, E energy input, L labour input, M materials, K capital input, and t denotes a technology index so that we can also define technical change as $\partial f(\cdot)/\partial t$.

According to duality theory, under the assumption that firms competitively minimize the cost of production subject to producing a given amount of output, technology can also be described by a cost function of the form

$$C = C(P_E, P_L, P_M, P_K, t) \qquad (2.2)$$

where C is total cost and P_i $(i = E, L, M, K)$ are factor prices.

Applying Shephard's lemma [see Diewert (1971)] to equation (2.2), we can derive the input demand functions, in terms of cost shares, as follows

$$s_i = \frac{\partial C(\cdot)}{\partial \ln P_i}, \ i = E, L, M, K \qquad (2.3)$$

These cost share equations can then be used to investigate the demand for aggregate energy and the substitutability/complementarity relation between energy and other aggregate inputs (in particular, labour, materials, and capital). They can also be used to calculate the rate of technical change, measures of the effect of technical change on each aggregate input [as in Diewert and Wales (1992)], and the elasticities of substitution for the aggregate inputs E, L, M, and K. See, for example, Feng and Serletis (2008) for more details.

2.2.1   *The Energy Submodel*

Our objective is the investigation of interfuel substitution between crude oil, coal, natural gas, and electricity. In doing so, we follow Fuss (1977) and assume that the production function (2.1) is homothetically weakly separable in energy, so that it can be written as

$$Y = f(E(E_1, \cdots, E_n), L, M, K, t) \qquad (2.4)$$

where $E(\cdot)$ is a homothetic function over n energy types, $E_1, \cdots, E_n$, representing the total energy measure.

Using duality theory of cost and production functions, Shephard (1953) showed that the cost function corresponding to the homothetically weakly separable production function in (2.2) is also weakly separable, as follows

$$C = C(P_E(P_{E_1}, \cdots, P_{E_n}), P_L, P_M, P_K, t) \qquad (2.5)$$

where $P_E(\cdot)$ is an energy price aggregator function, often interpreted as the price per unit of energy. The energy price aggregator function, $P_E(\cdot)$, can be represented by an arbitrary unit cost function similar to that used in equation (2.2).

Again, applying Shephard's lemma to $P_E(\cdot)$, we can obtain the demand functions for the individual energy types, $E_1, \cdots, E_n$, in terms of shares in the cost of the energy aggregate, $E(\cdot)$, as follows

$$s_{E_i} = \frac{\partial \ln P_E(\cdot)}{\partial \ln P_{E_i}}, \ i = 1, \cdots, n \qquad (2.6)$$

These cost share equations can then be used to investigate the demand for individual energy types, $E_1, \cdots, E_n$, and estimate the structure of substitution among the different energy types.

2.2.2 The Translog Energy Price Aggregator Function

So far, most of the literature on energy demand and interfuel substitution employed locally flexible functional forms for either (2.2), (2.5), or both — see, for example, Fuss (1977), Pindyck (1979), and Jones (1995). These forms provide the capability to approximate systems resulting from a broad class of generating functions and also to attain arbitrary elasticities of substitution although at only one point (that is, locally). However, although locally flexible functional forms provide arbitrary elasticity estimates at the point of approximation, they gain this precision at the expense of giving up global regularity. There is also some evidence that these models fail to meet the regularity conditions for cost minimization in large regions.

In this chapter, and in order to be consistent with the existing empirical literature, we investigate energy demand issues and interfuel substitution based on the use of the translog flexible functional form, introduced by Christensen *et al.* (1975). In doing so, we pay explicit attention to the theoretical regularity conditions of positivity, monotonicity, and curvature. In fact, motivated by the widespread practice of ignoring the theoretical regularity conditions, we will estimate the model subject to theoretical regularity using methods developed by Diewert and Wales (1987) and Ryan and Wales (2000).

The translog aggregator function is written as

$$\ln P_E = \ln \alpha_0 + \sum_{i=1}^{n} \beta_i \ln P_{E_i} + \frac{1}{2} \sum_{i=1}^{n} \sum_{j=1}^{n} \gamma_{ij} \ln P_{E_i} \ln P_{E_j} \qquad (2.7)$$

where i, j are individual energy types, and P_{E_i} is the price of energy type i. The assumption that the aggregator function is homogeneous of degree one in prices, requires that the following parameter restrictions

$$\sum_{i=1}^{n} \beta_i = 1$$

$$\qquad (2.8)$$

$$\sum_{i=1}^{n} \gamma_{ij} = \sum_{i=1}^{n} \gamma_{ji} = 0$$

be satisfied by the energy price aggregator function, $P_E(\cdot)$. Applying Shephard's lemma to the translog price aggregator function (2.7), we obtain the demand functions for the individual energy types, $E_1, \cdots, E_n$, in terms of shares in aggregate energy expenditure, as

$$s_{E_i} = \frac{\partial \ln P_E(\cdot)}{\partial \ln P_{E_i}} = \beta_i + \sum_{j=1}^{n} \gamma_{ij} \ln P_{E_j}, \ i,j = 1, \cdots, n \qquad (2.9)$$

In our case of four inputs, oil (o), natural gas (g), coal (c), and electricity (e), the above equation written out in full is

$$s_{E_o} = \beta_o + \gamma_{oo} \ln P_{E_o} + \gamma_{og} \ln P_{E_g} + \gamma_{oc} \ln P_{E_c} + \gamma_{oe} \ln P_{E_e}$$

$$s_{E_g} = \beta_g + \gamma_{go} \ln P_{E_o} + \gamma_{gg} \ln P_{E_g} + \gamma_{gc} \ln P_{E_c} + \gamma_{ge} \ln P_{E_e}$$

$$\qquad (2.10)$$

$$s_{E_c} = \beta_c + \gamma_{co} \ln P_{E_o} + \gamma_{cg} \ln P_{E_g} + \gamma_{cc} \ln P_{E_c} + \gamma_{ce} \ln P_{E_e}$$

$$s_{E_e} = \beta_e + \gamma_{eo} \ln P_{E_o} + \gamma_{eg} \ln P_{E_g} + \gamma_{ec} \ln P_{E_c} + \gamma_{ee} \ln P_{E_e}$$

The cost share equations in (2.10) form the basis of the empirical estimation in this chapter. Notice that in the absence of symmetry there are 20 parameters to estimate, 5 in each of the four share equations. The imposition, however, of the 6 symmetry restrictions, $\gamma_{og} = \gamma_{go}$, $\gamma_{oc} = \gamma_{co}$,

$\gamma_{oe} = \gamma_{eo}$, $\gamma_{gc} = \gamma_{cg}$, $\gamma_{ge} = \gamma_{eg}$, and $\gamma_{ce} = \gamma_{ec}$, reduces the number of parameters to 14.

Moreover, homogeneity of degree 1 in prices requires that conditions (2.8) are satisfied. In our four-variable (o, g, c, and e), symmetry-constrained framework, the restrictions corresponding to (2.8) can be written as

$$\beta_o + \beta_g + \beta_c + \beta_e = 1$$
$$\gamma_{oo} + \gamma_{og} + \gamma_{oc} + \gamma_{oe} = 0$$
$$\gamma_{og} + \gamma_{gg} + \gamma_{gc} + \gamma_{ge} = 0$$
$$\gamma_{oc} + \gamma_{gc} + \gamma_{cc} + \gamma_{ce} = 0$$
$$\gamma_{oe} + \gamma_{ge} + \gamma_{ce} + \gamma_{ee} = 0$$

These additional restrictions reduce the number of free parameters to 9.

2.2.3 Theoretical Regularity

As required by neoclassical microeconomic theory, the translog aggregator function has to satisfy certain regularity conditions such as, positivity, monotonicity, and curvature. Positivity requires that the cost function be positive for all the data observations. Monotonicity requires that the first order derivatives of the cost function, which correspond to input demands, be nonnegative. Curvature requires that the cost function is a concave function of prices or, equivalently, that the Hessian matrix of the cost function, $\boldsymbol{H}$, be negative semidefinite.

As shown by Diewert and Wales (1987), the Hessian matrix, $\boldsymbol{H}$, is negative semidefinite if and only if the following matrix is negative semidefinite

$$\boldsymbol{G} = \boldsymbol{\Gamma} - \underline{\boldsymbol{s}} + \boldsymbol{ss}'$$

where $\boldsymbol{\Gamma} = [\gamma_{ij}]$, $\boldsymbol{s} = (s_1, \cdots, s_n)$ is the share vector, and $\underline{\boldsymbol{s}}$ is the $n \times n$ diagonal matrix which has the share vector $\boldsymbol{s}$ on the main diagonal.

At the reference point (where all prices are set to one), the $\boldsymbol{G}$ matrix can be simplified as follows

$$\boldsymbol{G}_{ij} = \gamma_{ij} + \beta_i\beta_j - \delta_{ij}\beta_i$$

with $\delta_{ij} = 1$ if $i = j$ and 0 otherwise. Local concavity (at the reference point) can be imposed as in Ryanand Wales (2000) and Feng and Serletis (2008), by setting $\boldsymbol{H} = -\boldsymbol{KK}'$, as follows

$$\gamma_{ij} + \beta_i\beta_j - \delta_{ij}\beta_i = \left(-\boldsymbol{KK}'\right)_{ij}, \; i,j = 1, \cdots, n$$

where $\boldsymbol{K}$ is a lower triangular matrix. Since the elements of any row of the $\boldsymbol{\Gamma}$ matrix add up to zero, as implied by equations (2.8), only $(n-1) \times (n-1)$ elements of $\boldsymbol{\Gamma}$ are linearly independent. Therefore, the $\boldsymbol{K}$ matrix must be of dimension $(n-1) \times (n-1)$ as well.

It can easily be shown that in our case with four fuels $(n = 4)$, $i = o, g, c, e$, the γ_{ij} elements of $\boldsymbol{\Gamma}$ can be replaced by the k_{ij} elements of $\boldsymbol{K}$ as follows [see Feng and Serletis (2008) for more details]

$$
\begin{aligned}
\gamma_{oo} &= -\left(k_{go} + k_{co}\right)^2 + \beta_o - \beta_o^2 \\
\gamma_{og} &= \left(k_{go} + k_{co}\right) k_{go} - \beta_o \beta_g \\
\gamma_{oc} &= \left(k_{go} + k_{co}\right) k_{co} - \beta_o \beta_c \\
\gamma_{gg} &= -k_{go}^2 - k_{co}^2 + \beta_g - \beta_g^2 \\
\gamma_{gc} &= -k_{go} k_{co} + k_{cg}^2 - \beta_g \beta_c \\
\gamma_{cc} &= -\left(k_{co}^2 + k_{cg}^2\right) + \beta_c - \beta_c^2
\end{aligned}
\tag{2.11}
$$

which guarantee concavity of the cost function at the reference point and may also induce concavity of the cost function at other data points. Clearly, the flexibility of the translog specification is not destroyed, because the $n(n-1)/2$ elements of $\boldsymbol{K}$ just replace the $n(n-1)/2$ elements of $\boldsymbol{\Gamma}$ in the estimation.

2.3   Empirical Modelling

In order to implement the share equation system (2.9) empirically, a stochastic component ε_{E_i} is added to each share equation, $i = o, g, c, e$, and we assume that the error vector $\varepsilon_E = \left(\varepsilon_{E_o}, \varepsilon_{E_g}, \varepsilon_{E_c}, \varepsilon_{E_e}\right)$ is multivariate normally distributed with zero mean and the 4×4 error covariance matrix $\boldsymbol{\Omega}$. Hence the share equation system (2.10) can be written as

$$
s_{E_o} = \beta_o + \gamma_{oo} \ln P_{E_o} + \gamma_{og} \ln P_{E_g} + \gamma_{oc} \ln P_{E_c} + \gamma_{oe} \ln P_{E_e} + \varepsilon_{E_o}
$$

$$
s_{E_g} = \beta_g + \gamma_{go} \ln P_{E_o} + \gamma_{gg} \ln P_{E_g} + \gamma_{gc} \ln P_{E_c} + \gamma_{ge} \ln P_{E_e} + \varepsilon_{E_g}
$$

$$
\tag{2.12}
$$

$$
s_{E_c} = \beta_c + \gamma_{co} \ln P_{E_o} + \gamma_{cg} \ln P_{E_g} + \gamma_{cc} \ln P_{E_c} + \gamma_{ce} \ln P_{E_e} + \varepsilon_{E_c}
$$

$$
s_{E_e} = \beta_e + \gamma_{eo} \ln P_{E_o} + \gamma_{eg} \ln P_{E_g} + \gamma_{ec} \ln P_{E_c} + \gamma_{ee} \ln P_{E_e} + \varepsilon_{E_e}
$$

It is also to be noted that the shares sum to unity and the random disturbances corresponding to the four share equations sum to zero. This yields a singular covariance matrix of errors. Barten (1969) has shown that full information maximum likelihood estimates of the parameters can be obtained by arbitrarily deleting any one equation; the resulting estimates are invariant with respect to the equation deleted. For example, deleting the 4th equation, our four-equation, symmetry-constrained framework, with the homogeneity restrictions imposed can be written as follows

$$
\begin{aligned}
s_{E_o} &= \beta_o + \gamma_{oo} \ln P_{E_o} + \gamma_{og} \ln P_{E_g} + \gamma_{oc} \ln P_{E_c} \\
&\quad - (\gamma_{oo} + \gamma_{og} + \gamma_{oc}) \ln P_{E_e} + \varepsilon_{E_o} \\
s_{E_g} &= \beta_g + \gamma_{og} \ln P_{E_o} + \gamma_{gg} \ln P_{E_g} + \gamma_{gc} \ln P_{E_c} \\
&\quad - (\gamma_{og} + \gamma_{gg} + \gamma_{gc}) \ln P_{E_e} + \varepsilon_{E_g} \quad\quad (2.13) \\
s_{E_c} &= \beta_c + \gamma_{oc} \ln P_{E_o} + \gamma_{gc} \ln P_{E_g} + \gamma_{cc} \ln P_{E_c} \\
&\quad - (\gamma_{oc} + \gamma_{gc} + \gamma_{cc}) \ln P_{E_e} + \varepsilon_{E_c}
\end{aligned}
$$

or, equivalently,

$$
\begin{aligned}
s_{E_o} &= \beta_o + \gamma_{oo} \ln \left(P_{E_o}/P_{E_e} \right) \\
&\quad + \gamma_{og} \ln \left(P_{E_g}/P_{E_e} \right) + \gamma_{oc} \ln \left(P_{E_c}/P_{E_e} \right) + \varepsilon_{E_o} \\
s_{E_g} &= \beta_g + \gamma_{og} \ln \left(P_{E_o}/P_{E_e} \right) \\
&\quad + \gamma_{gg} \ln \left(P_{E_g}/P_{E_e} \right) + \gamma_{gc} \ln \left(P_{E_c}/P_{E_e} \right) + \varepsilon_{E_g} \quad\quad (2.14) \\
s_{E_c} &= \beta_c + \gamma_{oc} \ln \left(P_{E_o}/P_{E_e} \right) \\
&\quad + \gamma_{gc} \ln \left(P_{E_g}/P_{E_e} \right) + \gamma_{cc} \ln \left(P_{E_c}/P_{E_e} \right) + \varepsilon_{E_c}
\end{aligned}
$$

Parameter estimates of the fourth (omitted) share equation can be obtained from the imposed linear homogeneity restrictions as follows

$$
\begin{aligned}
\beta_e &= 1 - \beta_o - \beta_g - \beta_c \\
\gamma_{oe} &= - (\gamma_{oo} + \gamma_{og} + \gamma_{oc}) \\
\gamma_{ge} &= - (\gamma_{og} + \gamma_{gg} + \gamma_{gc}) \\
\gamma_{ce} &= - (\gamma_{oc} + \gamma_{gc} + \gamma_{cc}) \\
\gamma_{ee} &= - (\gamma_{oe} + \gamma_{ge} + \gamma_{ce}) \\
&= \gamma_{oo} + \gamma_{gg} + \gamma_{cc} + 2 (\gamma_{og} + \gamma_{oc} + \gamma_{gc})
\end{aligned}
$$

Finally, when local curvature is imposed, we replace γ_{oo}, γ_{og}, γ_{oc}, γ_{gg}, γ_{gc}, and γ_{cc} in system (2.14) by the expressions on the right side of (2.11), thereby estimating the elements of the $\boldsymbol{K}$ matrix instead of those of the $\boldsymbol{\Gamma}$ matrix. The elements of $\boldsymbol{\Gamma}$ could then be recovered from (2.11).

2.3.1 *Elasticities*

Under the assumption of a constant aggregate energy expenditure (allowing emphasis on interfuel substitution alone), the Allen partial elasticities of substitution between inputs i and j, σ_{ij}, are computed as

$$\sigma_{ij}^a = \frac{C \cdot C_{ij}}{C_i \cdot C_j}, \quad i, j = 1, \cdots, n$$

where C is the cost function and the i, j subscripts refer to first and second partial derivatives of C with respect to input prices. See Uzawa (1964) and Diewert (1974) for more details.

In our four-variable (o, g, c, and e) framework, the Allen elasticities of substitution can be calculated as follows

$$\sigma_{ii}^a = \frac{\gamma_{ii} + s_{E_i}^2 - s_{E_i}}{s_{E_i}^2}, \quad i = o, g, c, e$$

$$\sigma_{ij}^a = \frac{\gamma_{ij} + s_{E_i} s_{E_j}}{s_{E_i} s_{E_j}}, \quad i, j = o, g, c, e \ \ i \# j$$

If $\sigma_{ij}^a > 0$ (that is, if increasing the jth price increases the optimal quantity of input i), we say that inputs i and j are Allen-Uzawa (net) substitutes. If $\sigma_{ij}^a < 0$, they are Allen-Uzawa (net) complements.

The Allen elasticity of substitution is the traditional measure and has been employed to measure substitution behavior and structural instability in a variety of contexts. However, when there are more than two inputs the Allen elasticity may be uninformative — see, for example, Blackorby and Russell (1989). With more than two inputs the relationship becomes complex and depends on things like the direction taken towards the point of approximation. In that case the Morishima elasticity of substitution, σ_{ij}^m,

$$\sigma_{ij}^m = s_{E_j} \left(\sigma_{ij}^a - \sigma_{jj}^a \right), \quad i, j = o, g, c, e$$

where s_{E_j} is the share of input j, is the correct measure of substitution elasticity. Notice that the Morishima elasticity looks at the impact on the ratio of two inputs, x_i / x_j. That is, we hold the price of input i fixed and examine how changes in the price of input j affect the quantity ratio, x_i / x_j. Inputs will be Morishima complements (substitutes) if an increase in the price of j causes x_i / x_j to decrease (increase).

Moreover, since the own-price (η_{ii}) and cross-price (η_{ij}) elasticities of demand are given by

$$\eta_{ij} = s_j \sigma_{ij}^a, \quad i,j = 1, \cdots, n$$

in our framework, the own- and cross-price elasticities of demand for individual energy types can be calculated as follows

$$\eta_{ii} = s_{E_i} \sigma_{ii}^a, \quad i = o, g, c, e$$

$$\eta_{ij} = s_{E_j} \sigma_{ij}^a, \quad i,j = o, g, c, e \ \ i \# j$$

2.3.2 *Separability Testing*

We also test for weak separability with the objective of discovering the structure of the functional form. The tests that we carry out for weak separability are based on the assumption that the translog functional form is a second-order approximation to an arbitrary aggregator function. This approach has been suggested by Denny and Fuss (1977) and provides a less restrictive test for separability than the Berndt and Christensen (1973) framework, which is based on the maintained hypothesis that the translog specification is exact. At an intuitive level, the Berndt and Christensen exact test is a test for global separability, while the Denny and Fuss (1977) approximate test is a tests for local separability (exact separability only at the point of expansion and approximate separability elsewhere).

As in Serletis (1987), to derive our approximate tests for weak separability, we consider the separability restrictions associated with restrictions on the functional form. As shown in the table below, with four variables, three separability patterns exist: the separability of two variables from the other two variables (resulting in six ways of choosing a group of two variables to be separable from the other two variables); the symmetric separability of two variables from the other two variables (resulting in three ways of placing two variables in each group); and the separability of three variables from the fourth (resulting in four possible ways with three variables in one group). These possibilities and the corresponding parametric restrictions are shown below

Separability pattern	Parametric restrictions
$f(g(\ln x_i, \ln x_j), \ln x_k, \ln x_l)$	$\beta_i/\beta_j = \gamma_{ik}/\gamma_{jk} = \gamma_{il}/\gamma_{jl}$
$f(g(\ln x_i, \ln x_j), h(\ln x_k, \ln x_l))$	$\beta_i/\beta_j = \gamma_{ik}/\gamma_{jk} = \gamma_{il}/\gamma_{jl}$
	$\beta_k/\beta_l = \gamma_{ik}/\gamma_{il} = \gamma_{jk}/\gamma_{jl}$
$f(g(\ln x_i, \ln x_j, \ln x_k), \ln x_l)$	$\beta_i/\beta_j = \gamma_{il}/\gamma_{jl} = \gamma_{il}/\gamma_{kl}$
	$\beta_j/\beta_k = \gamma_{jl}/\gamma_{kl}$

For each null hypothesis, we express the weak separability conditions in terms of the free parameters of the model, and calculate the Wald test statistic which is distributed asymptotically as a chi-square with degrees of freedom equal to the number of independent parametric restrictions. The Wald test statistic is asymptotically equivalent to the likelihood ratio test statistic, but the Wald test, unlike the likelihood-ratio test, does not require the numerical minimization of both constrained and unconstrained models.

2.4 The United States Data

We investigate interfuel substitution in the United States economy using annual data from the Energy Information Administration (EIA) over the 1960 to 2007 period, a total of 48 annual observations $(T = 48)$. In doing so, we estimate a four-fuel model $(n = 4)$ for petroleum products (o), natural gas (g), electricity (e), and coal (c). Individual fuel (total final) consumption data are obtained from the Primary Energy Consumption by Source (1949-2007) table. The price series for oil, natural gas, and coal are obtained from the Fossil Fuel Production Prices (1949-2007) table and the electricity price is from the Average Retail Prices of Electricity (1960-2007) table.

Because of aggregation errors in estimating a national level model, and because interfuel substitution is different for different sectors of use, we also provide a sectoral investigation, using data for the industrial, commercial, residential, and electricity-generation sectors of the U.S. economy. Data limitations, however, make it impossible to use a four-fuel model for all sectors and over the same sample period as with the national-level data. We thus use a four-fuel model (o, g, e, c) for the industrial sector, a three-fuel model (o, g, e) for the commercial and residential sectors (given that coal consumption is close to zero in these sectors), and a three-fuel model (o, g, c)

for the electricity-generation sector (given that electricity is an output and not an input in this sector). Also, because of data limitations, the sample period for the industrial sector is from 1968 to 2007 ($T = 40$); for the residential sector from 1967 to 2007 ($T = 41$); for the commercial sector from 1978 to 2007 ($T = 30$); and for the electricity generation sector from 1973 to 2007 ($T = 35$).

For the purpose of the sectoral analysis, consumed quantities of oil, natural gas, electricity, and coal are obtained from the Energy Consumption by Sector (1949–2007) tables. Prices for natural gas and electricity for the industrial, commercial, and residential sectors are from the Natural Gas Prices by Sector (1967-2007) and Average Retail Prices of Electricity (1960-2007) tables, respectively. The coal price series from the Coal Prices (1949-2007) table and the composite price of oil, from the Crude Oil Refiner Acquisition Costs (1968-2007) table, are used as the representative coal and oil prices, respectively, in the industrial sector. The retail gasoline price, from the Nominal Retail Gasoline Price (1949-2007) table, is used as a proxy for the price of oil in the residential sector and the composite price of gasoline (all types), found in the U.S. City Average Retail Gasoline Price (1978-2007) table, is used as a proxy for the price of petroleum products in the commercial sector. Finally, for the electricity generation sector, the prices of the corresponding energy inputs are from the Cost of Fossil-Fuel Receipts at Electric Generating Plants (1973-2007) table.

All quantity data are expressed in billion Btu and all prices are real or converted to real prices using the GDP implicit price deflator (2000 = 1.00). Since petroleum products, natural gas, electricity, and coal are measured in different units, prices are converted to dollars per billion Btu, using the EIA conversion rates based on U.S. consumption in 2007, as follows

Crude oil:	1 Barrel = 5,800,000 Btu
Gasoline:	1 Gallon = 124,000 Btu
Natural gas:	1 Cubic foot = 1,028 Btu
Electricity:	1 Kilowatt hour = 3,412 Btu
Coal:	1 Short ton = 20,169,000 Btu

2.5 Empirical Evidence

All estimations are performed in TSP/GiveWin (version 4.5) using the LSQ procedure. As results are sensitive to the initial parameter values, to avoid being caught in local minima and in order to achieve global convergence, we randomly generate sets of initial parameter values and choose the starting values that lead to the highest value of the log likelihood function. The parameter estimates of the unrestricted models (that is, the models estimated without the curvature conditions imposed) are reported in Tables 2.1-2.5, with p-values in parentheses. The log likelihood values are also reported, together with the number of positivity, monotonicity, and curvature violations, checked as in Feng and Serletis (2008). In particular, positivity is checked by checking if the estimated energy price aggregator function is positive. Monotonicity is checked by direct computation of the values of the first gradient vector of the estimated aggregator function with respect to p. Curvature requires the Hessian matrix of the aggregator function to be negative semidefinite and is checked by examining the eigenvalues of the Hessian matrix provided that the monotonicity condition holds. It requires that these eigenvalues be nonpositive.

As can be seen in Tables 2.1-2.5, although positivity and monotonicity are satisfied at all sample observations and for all five data sets, curvature is violated for all observations with the industrial sector and electricity-generation sector data and for 31 out of the 48 observations with the national-level data. Curvature, however, is satisfied at all observations with the commercial and residential sector data. Because regularity has not been attained (by luck) for any of the national-level data and the industrial and electricity-generation sector data, we follow Diewert and Wales (1987), Ryan and Wales (2000), and Feng and Serletis (2008) and estimate these models by imposing local curvature, using the procedure discussed earlier.

As noted by Ryan and Wales (2000), however, the ability of locally flexible models to satisfy curvature at sample observations other than the point of approximation depends on the choice of the approximation point. Thus, we estimated each of these models a number of times equal to the number of observations (each time picking a different approximation point), and report results for the best approximation point (best in the sense of satisfying the curvature conditions at the largest number of observations). The results of the curvature-constrained models are presented in the second column of Tables 2.1, 2.2, and 2.5, in the same fashion as those for the unconstrained models in the first column of these tables.

The imposition of local curvature, at the best approximation point, has a significant impact on the model with the national-level data (see Table 2.1), as it reduces the number of curvature violations from 31 to 13, without

Table 2.1   Parameter Estimates with National Level Data

Inputs:

o = oil
g = natural gas
e = electricity
c = coal

Parameter	Unrestricted	Local curvature imposed
β_o	.325 (.000)	.339 (.000)
β_g	.057 (.000)	.065 (.000)
β_e	.551 (.000)	.530 (.000)
γ_{oo}	.225 (.000)	.192 (.000)
γ_{og}	−.026 (.000)	−.027 (.000)
γ_{oe}	−.179 (.000)	−.138 (.000)
γ_{gg}	.035 (.000)	.058 (.000)
γ_{ge}	−.008 (.000)	−.031 (.000)
γ_{ee}	.204 (.000)	.191 (.000)
$\mathrm{Log}L$	496.389	441.305
Positivity violations	0	0
Monotonicity violations	0	0
Curvature violations	31	13
Normalization year	1998	1967

Note: Sample period, annual data 1960-2007 ($T = 48$). Numbers in parentheses are p-values.

any induced violations of monotonicity. In the case of the industrial sector data (see Table 2.2), the effect is not as significant as the number of curvature violations declines only from 40 to 32. With the electricity-generation sector data, however, the imposition of local curvature reduces the number of curvature violations from 35 to 3 (see Table 2.5), achieving almost full regularity. A comparison, however, of the log likelihood values for both the unconstrained and constrained models, indicates that imposition of the local curvature constraints has a significant influence on the flexibility of the models, as the log likelihood values decrease from 496.389 to 441.305 with the national-level data, from 364.784 to 353.776 with the industrial sector data, and from 125.144 to 99.900 with the electricity-generation sector data. With this in mind, in what follows we discuss the price elasticities as well as the Allen and Morishima elasticities of substitution based on the curvature-constrained models for the national level data and the industrial

Table 2.2   Parameter Estimates with Industrial Sector Data

		Local
Parameter	Unrestricted	curvature imposed

Inputs:

o = oil
g = natural gas
e = electricity
c = coal

Parameter	Unrestricted	Local curvature imposed
β_o	.294 (.000)	.291 (.000)
β_g	.142 (.000)	.167 (.000)
β_e	.522 (.000)	.493 (.000)
γ_{oo}	.169 (.001)	.204 (.000)
γ_{og}	−.009 (.091)	−.035 (.000)
γ_{oe}	−.159 (.000)	−.161 (.000)
γ_{gg}	.059 (.000)	.049 (.000)
γ_{ge}	−.025 (.024)	.038 (.000)
γ_{ee}	.229 (.000)	.082 (.002)
Log$L$	364.784	353.776
Positivity violations	0	0
Monotonicity violations	0	0
Curvature violations	40	32
Normalization year	2005	1998

Note: Sample period, annual data 1968-2007 ($T = 40$). Numbers in parentheses are p-values.

and electricity-generation sector data. For the commercial and residential sector data, we use the unconstrained model, since it can guarantee inference consistent with the theory, without compromising the flexibility of the functional form.

The own-and cross-price elasticities (calculated at the mean of the data, based on the formulas presented earlier) are shown in panel A of Tables 2.6-2.10 along with their p-values. The p-values have been computed by linearizing the elasticity formulas around the estimated parameter values and then by using the standard formulas for the variance of linear functions of random variables. The own-price elasticities (η_{ii}) are all negative (as predicted by the theory), with the absolute values of these elasticities (in general) being less than 1, which indicates that the demands for all fuels are inelastic. The residential sector presents the only exception with own-price elasticity for oil, η_{oo}, being −1.002. The negativeness of the own-price

Table 2.3   Parameter Estimates with Commercial Sector Data

Inputs:

o = oil
g = natural gas
e = electricity

Parameter	Unrestricted	Local curvature imposed
β_o	.063 (.000)	
β_g	.102 (.000)	
γ_{oo}	−.001 (.972)	
γ_{og}	−.016 (.019)	
γ_{gg}	.051 (.000)	
Log$L$	185.259	
Positivity violations	0	
Monotonicity violations	0	
Curvature violations	0	
Normalization year	2006	

Note: Sample period, annual data 1978-2007 $(T = 30)$. Numbers in parentheses are p -values.

Table 2.4   Parameter Estimates with Residential Sector Data

Inputs:

o = oil
g = natural gas
e = electricity

Parameter	Unrestricted	Local curvature imposed
β_o	.109 (.000)	
β_g	.129 (.000)	
γ_{oo}	−.020 (.670)	
γ_{og}	−.036 (.001)	
γ_{gg}	.062 (.000)	
Log$L$	198.204	
Positivity violations	0	
Monotonicity violations	0	
Curvature violations	0	
Normalization year	2006	

Note: Sample period, annual data 1967-2007 $(T = 41)$. Numbers in parentheses are p -values.

Table 2.5　Parameter Estimates with Electricity Generation Sector Data

Inputs:

o = oil
g = natural gas
c = coal

Parameter	Unrestricted	curvature imposed
β_o	.153 (.000)	.098 (.000)
β_g	.116 (.000)	.208 (.000)
γ_{oo}	.063 (.001)	.045 (.410)
γ_{og}	−.101 (.000)	−.026 (.158)
γ_{gg}	.290 (.000)	
Log$L$	125.144	99.900
Positivity violations	0	0
Monotonicity violations	0	0
Curvature violations	35	3
Normalization year	1975	1976

Note: Sample period, annual data 1973-2007 ($T = 35$). Numbers in parentheses are p -values.

elasticities theoretically validates the use of the translog model. For the cross-price elasticities (η_{ij}), economic theory does not predict any signs.

From the point of view of energy policy, the measurement of the elasticities of substitution among the different fuels is of prime importance. As already noted, there are currently two methods employed for calculating the partial elasticity of substitution between two variables, the Allen and Morishima. The Allen elasticity of substitution is the traditional measure and has been employed to measure substitution behavior and structural instability in a variety of contexts. However, when there are more than two inputs, the Allen elasticity may be uninformative — see, for example, Blackorby and Russell (1989). For two inputs the relationship is unambiguous: the inputs must be substitutes. When there are more than two inputs, the relationship becomes complex and depends on the direction taken toward the point of approximation. In that case the Morishima elasticity of substitution is the correct measure of substitution elasticity. The Morishima elasticity examines how changes in the price of input j (holding the price of input i fixed) affects the quantity ratio x_i/x_j. Inputs will be

Morishima complements (substitutes) if an increase in the price of j causes x_i/x_j to decrease (increase).

We report the Allen elasticities of substitution (calculated at the mean of the data, based on the formula presented earlier), together with p-values, in panel B of Tables 2.6-2.10, so that other researchers can compare with prior estimates and in order to test the validity of our models. In particular, we expect the diagonal terms, representing the Allen own-elasticities of substitution for the different fuels to be negative. This expectation is clearly achieved. Although the diagonal terms in Tables 2.6-2.10 are all negative, some of the estimates reported are large (in absolute terms). This is, for example, the case of coal in the industrial sector (see Table 2.7) and the case of oil in the commercial and residential sectors (see Tables 2.8 and 2.9, respectively). This can be explained by writing σ_{ij}^a as $\sigma_{ij}^a = \eta_{ij}/s_j$, indicating that σ_{ij}^a is large when the cost share s_j is small. However, because the Allen elasticity of substitution produces ambiguous results off-diagonal, we use the Morishima elasticity of substitution to investigate the substitutability/complementarity relation between fuels.

The asymmetrical Morishima elasticities of substitution — the correct measures of substitution — as documented in Tables 2.6-2.10 (again elasticities at the mean of the data are reported based on the formula presented earlier), are all positive (although small), suggesting substitutability among the different fuels. The only exception is the Morishima elasticity of substitution between coal (c) and natural gas (g), σ_{cg}^m, with the industrial sector data, being $-.383$ with a p-value of .000. It represents the percentage change in the c/g ratio when the relative price p_g/p_c is changed by changing p_g and holding p_c constant. Moreover, although most Morishima elasticities of substitution are less than unity, there is also strong evidence of substitutability in the industrial sector between coal and electricity and natural gas and electricity in response to changes in the price of electricity; the Morishima elasticities of substitution are $\sigma_{ce}^m = 1.567$ (with a p-value of .000) and $\sigma_{ge}^m = 1.093$ (with a p-value of .000), respectively. There is also strong evidence of substitutability between oil and electricity in the commercial and residential sectors, irrespective of whether the price of oil or the price of electricity changes. In particular, in the commercial sector, $\sigma_{eo}^m = 1.032$ (with a p-value of .000) and $\sigma_{oe}^m = 1.214$ (with a p-value of .000) and in the residential sector, $\sigma_{eo}^m = 1.217$ (with a p-value of .000) and $\sigma_{oe}^m = 1.439$ (with a p-value of .000).

Table 2.6   Elasticities with National Level Data

A. Own- and cross-price elasticities

Factor i	η_{io}	η_{ig}	η_{ie}	η_{ic}
o	$-.116(.000)$	$.036(.002)$	$.081(.001)$	$-.001(.005)$
g	$.133(.002)$	$-.347(.000)$	$.143(.001)$	$.070(.000)$
e	$.072(.001)$	$.034(.001)$	$-.126(.000)$	$.019(.000)$
c	$-.011(.005)$	$.112(.000)$	$.124(.000)$	$-.224(.000)$

B. Allen elasticities of substitution

Factor i	σ^a_{io}	σ^a_{ig}	σ^a_{ie}	σ^a_{ic}
o	$-.299\ (.000)$	$.344\ (.002)$	$.185\ (.001)$	$-.028\ (.006)$
g		$-3.258\ (.000)$	$.326\ (.001)$	$1.050\ (.000)$
e			$-.287\ (.000)$	$.283\ (.000)$
c				$-3.335\ (.000)$

C. Morishima elasticities of substitution

Factor i	σ^m_{io}	σ^m_{ig}	σ^m_{ie}	σ^m_{ic}
o		$.384\ (.000)$	$.207\ (.000)$	$.223\ (.000)$
g	$.249\ (.000)$		$.269\ (.000)$	$.295\ (.000)$
e	$.188\ (.000)$	$.382\ (.000)$		$.244\ (.000)$
c	$.105\ (.000)$	$.459\ (.000)$	$.250\ (.000)$	

Note: Numbers in parantheses are p-values.

Finally, we report the weak separability test results in Tables 2.11-2.15, using the curvature-constrained models. At conventional significance levels, the p-values decisively reject all separability types with the national level data and the industrial and residential sector data (see Tables 2.11, 2.12, and 2.14). The only separability condition that our data cannot reject is the $[(o, e), g]$ weak separability restriction with the commercial sector data (see Table 2.13), suggesting that the cost-minimizing mix of oil and electricity is independent of the price of natural gas, and the $[(o, g), c]$, $[(o, c), g]$, and $[(g, c), o]$ weak separability restrictions with the electricity-generation sector data (see Table 2.15). In the case of the electricity-generation sector, technology and transportation costs provide the most plausible explanation for the weak separability patterns that we find, as most of the electricity generation facilities are either designed or build in a certain location to

Table 2.7   Elasticities with Industrial Sector Data

A. Own- and cross-price elasticities

Factor i	η_{io}	η_{ig}	η_{ie}	η_{ic}
o	$-.087$ (.000)	.044 (.011)	.010 (.663)	.033 (.000)
g	.131 (.011)	$-.496$ (.000)	.710 (.000)	$-.344$ (.000)
e	.009 (.663)	.226 (.000)	$-.383$ (.000)	.147 (.000)
c	.252 (.000)	$-.879$ (.000)	1.183 (.000)	$-.556$ (.000)

B. Allen elasticities of substitution

Factor i	σ_{io}^a	σ_{ig}^a	σ_{ie}^a	σ_{ic}^a
o	$-.222$ (.000)	.331 (.011)	.024 (.663)	.638 (.000)
g		-3.719 (.000)	1.693 (.000)	-6.589 (.000)
e			$-.914$ (.000)	2.824 (.000)
c				-10.642 (.000)

C. Morishima elasticities of substitution

Factor i	σ_{io}^m	σ_{ig}^m	σ_{ie}^m	σ_{ic}^m
o		.540 (.000)	.393 (.000)	.589 (.000)
g	.218 (.000)		1.093 (.000)	.211 (.000)
e	.097 (.000)	.722 (.000)		.703 (.000)
c	.339 (.000)	$-.383$ (.000)	1.567 (.000)	

Note: Numbers in parantheses are *p*-values.

operate using only one type of fuel as an input. For example, many of the coal-burning plants are built at mine mouth and cannot operate on natural gas; the same applies to natural gas-fired facilities, located near the well head.

Table 2.8   Elasticities with Commercial Sector Data

A. Own- and cross-price elasticities

Factor i	η_{io}	η_{ig}	η_{ie}	η_{ic}
o	$-.939$ (.005)	$-.141$ (.148)	1.080 (.009)	—
g	$-.122$ (.142)	$-.296$ (.000)	$.419$ (.000)	—
e	$.092$ (.010)	$.041$ (.000)	$-.134$ (.000)	—
c	—	—	—	—

B. Allen elasticities of substitution

Factor i	σ_{io}^a	σ_{ig}^a	σ_{ie}^a	σ_{ic}^a
o	-12.981 (.007)	-1.697 (.151)	1.280 (.009)	—
g		-3.565 (.000)	$.497$ (.000)	—
e			$-.158$ (.003)	—
c				—

C. Morishima elasticities of substitution

Factor i	σ_{io}^m	σ_{ig}^m	σ_{ie}^m	σ_{ic}^m
o		$.155$ (.000)	1.214 (.000)	—
g	$.816$ (.000)		$.553$ (.000)	—
e	1.032 (.000)	$.338$ (.000)		—
c	—	—	—	

Note: Numbers in parantheses are p-values.

Table 2.9   Elasticities with Residential Sector Data

A. Own- and cross-price elasticities

Factor i	η_{io}	η_{ig}	η_{ie}	η_{ic}
o	−1.002 (.003)	−.149 (.071)	1.151 (.005)	—
g	−.194 (.065)	−.313 (.000)	.507 (.000)	—
e	.214 (.005)	.072 (.000)	−.287 (.002)	—
c	—	—	—	—

B. Allen elasticities of substitution

Factor i	σ_{io}^a	σ_{ig}^a	σ_{ie}^a	σ_{ic}^a
o	−7.146 (.004)	−1.385 (.074)	1.532 (.005)	—
g		−2.903 (.000)	.675 (.000)	—
e			−.382 (.002)	—
c				—

C. Morishima elasticities of substitution

Factor i	σ_{io}^m	σ_{ig}^m	σ_{ie}^m	σ_{ic}^m
o		.163 (.000)	1.439 (.000)	—
g	.808 (.000)		.795 (.000)	—
e	1.217 (.000)	.386 (.000)		—
c	—	—	—	—

Note: Numbers in parantheses are *p*-values.

Table 2.10　Elasticities with Electricity Generation Sector Data

A.　Own- and cross-price elasticities

Factor i	η_{io}	η_{ig}	η_{ie}	η_{ic}
o	−.402 (.523)	−.020 (.920)	—	.422 (.000)
g	−.006 (.920)	−.136 (.000)	—	.142 (.000)
e	—	—	—	—
c	.059 (.000)	.064 (.000)	—	−.123 (.000)

B.　Allen elasticities of substitution

Factor i	σ_{io}^{a}	σ_{ig}^{a}	σ_{ie}^{a}	σ_{ic}^{a}
o	−4.553 (.516)	−.071 (.920)	—	.671 (.000)
g		−.482 (.000)	—	.227 (.000)
e	—	—	—	—
c				−.196 (.000)

C.　Morishima elasticities of substitution

Factor i	σ_{io}^{m}	σ_{ig}^{m}	σ_{ie}^{m}	σ_{ic}^{m}
o		.116 (.000)	—	.545 (.000)
g	.395 (.000)		—	.266 (.000)
e	—	—	—	—
c	461 (.000)	.201 (.000)	—	

Note:　Numbers in parantheses are *p*-values.

Table 2.11 Separability Hypotheses Tests with the National Level Data

Hypothesis	Degrees of freedom	$\mathcal{X}^2$	p-value
$[(o,g),e,c]$	2	5.792	.055
$[(o,e),g,c]$	2	17.523	.000
$[(o,c),g,e]$	2	7.612	.022
$[(g,e),o,c]$	2	10.130	.006
$[(g,c),o,e]$	2	8.658	.013
$[(e,c),o,g]$	2	17.967	.000
$[(o,g),(e,c)]$	4	18.987	.000
$[(o,e),(g,c)]$	4	26.197	.000
$[(o,c),(g,e)]$	4	23.656	.000
$[(o,g,e),c]$	3	18.802	.000
$[(g,e,c),o]$	3	19.525	.000
$[(o,g,c),e]$	3	15.318	.000
$[(o,e,c),g]$	3	12.291	.000

Table 2.12 Separability Hypotheses Tests with the Industrial Sector Data

Hypothesis	Degrees of freedom	$\mathcal{X}^2$	p-value
$[(o,g),e,c]$	2	161.614	.000
$[(o,e),g,c]$	2	43.376	.000
$[(o,c),g,e]$	2	51.362	.000
$[(g,e),o,c]$	2	43.576	.000
$[(g,c),o,e]$	2	8.758	.013
$[(e,c),o,g]$	2	61.747	.000
$[(o,g),(e,c)]$	4	188.408	.000
$[(o,e),(g,c)]$	4	78.448	.000
$[(o,c),(g,e)]$	4	56.772	.000
$[(o,g,e),c]$	3	181.880	.000
$[(g,e,c),o]$	3	77.808	.000
$[(o,g,c),e]$	3	139.246	.000
$[(o,e,c),g]$	3	47.144	.000

Table 2.13 Separability Hypotheses Tests
with the Commercial Sector Data

Hypothesis	Degrees of freedom	$\mathcal{X}^2$	p-value
$[(o,g),e]$	1	3.736	.053
$[(o,e),g]$	1	2.695	.101
$[(g,e),o]$	1	3.111	.078

Table 2.14 Separability Hypotheses Tests
with the Residential Sector Data

Hypothesis	Degrees of freedom	$\mathcal{X}^2$	p-value
$[(o,g),e]$	1	4.033	.044
$[(o,e),g]$	1	4.372	.036
$[(g,e),o]$	1	4.518	.033

Table 2.15 Separability Hypotheses Tests
with the Electricity-Generation Sector Data

Hypothesis	Degrees of freedom	$\mathcal{X}^2$	p-value
$[(o,g),c]$	1	.497	.481
$[(o,c),g]$	1	.147	.701
$[(g,c),o]$	1	.380	.538

2.6   Conclusions

We investigated interfuel substitution in the United States economy, taking a flexible functional form approach and using state-of-the-art advances in microeconometrics.   In particular, we employed a well-known flexible functional form, the locally flexible translog, introduced by Christensen *et al.* (1975), and employed in most of the empirical energy demand literature.   Moreover, motivated by the widespread practice of ignoring the theoretical regularity conditions, we estimated the model subject to theoretical regularity, using methods developed by Diewert and Wales (1987) and Ryan and Wales (2000), in an attempt to produce evidence consistent with theoretical regularity.   Moreover, in addition to investigating interfuel substitution possibilities in total U.S. energy demand, we also examined interfuel substitution possibilities in energy demand by sector (industrial, commercial, residential, and electricity-generation sectors).   We provided inference, and also a policy perspective, using parameter estimates that are in general consistent with the theoretical regularity conditions of neoclassical microeconomic theory.

Our evidence indicates that the interfuel elasticities of substitution are (in general) consistently below unity, revealing the limited ability to substitute one source of energy for another and suggesting that fossil fuels will continue to maintain their major role as a source of energy in the near future.

There are several problems that potentially could be addressed in productive future research.   First, in this chapter we have used the crude oil refiner acquisition cost as a measure of petroleum product prices.   This is the price paid to domestic producers in the United States and is highly correlated with the West Texas Intermediate (WTI) crude oil price at Chicago, although only a fraction of oil traded in the United States is contracted at WTI.   The robustness of our results to alternative petroleum product prices could thus be investigated.   Second, petroleum products include a wide variety of products with very different prices and end-use patterns.   For example, it includes distillate fuel oil, jet fuel, liquified petroleum gases, motor gasoline, residential fuel oil, and many other petroleum products.   Also, gasoline and diesel are used in transportation, with very little if any substitution in the short-run, and jet fuel is used in air travel.   However, there are no sectoral prices for these specific petroleum products.   If sectoral prices were available, then Divisia aggregation could be used, as in Berndt and Wood (1975).

Chapter 3

International Evidence on Sectoral Interfuel Substitution*

3.1 Introduction

In this chapter we investigate interfuel substitution at the sector level, using international time series data. In particular, we investigate interfuel substitution within the industrial, residential, transportation and electricity generation sectors for a number of OECD and non-OECD countries, since the structure of interfuel substitution is different for different sectors of use. We also use a locally flexible functional form to investigate interfuel substitution and to provide a comparison of our results with most of the existing empirical literature. In particular, we use the normalized quadratic (NQ) cost function, introduced by Diewert and Wales (1987), estimate the corresponding input-output equations subject to the theoretical regularity conditions using methods developed by Diewert and Wales (1987), and produce inference consistent with neoclassical microeconomic theory.

We use the most recent data (since 1980), published by the International Energy Agency (IEA), for a number of OECD and non-OECD countries (including China and India) for which reliable data are available. In particular, we provide evidence for six high-income countries (Canada, France, Japan, Italy, the United Kingdom and the United States), for five upper-middle to high-income economies (Poland, Hungary, Mexico, Turkey and Venezuela), and for four lower-middle to low-income economies (China, India, South Africa and Thailand).

*This article copyrighted and reprinted by permission from the International Association for Energy Economics, publishers of *The Energy Journal*. The article first appeared in *The Energy Journal*, Vol. 31, No. 4, pages 1-29, 2010. Visit *The Energy Journal* online at http://www.iaee.org/en/publications/journal.aspx"

The rest of the chapter is organized as follows. Section 3.2 briefly outlines the neoclassical energy problem. Section 3.3 discusses estimation issues while section 3.4 discusses the data. In section 3.5 we describe our estimation strategy and in section 3.6 provide a sectoral investigation, working with a number of countries and sectors for which data are available; data limitations make it impossible to deal with all sectors and for all countries. The final section concludes the chapter with suggestions for potentially productive future research.

3.2   Theoretical Foundations and the NQ Cost Function

As in Fuss (1977), we take the econometric approach, assuming a production function of the form

$$Y = f(E_1, E_2, ..., E_n, L, M, K, t) \tag{3.1}$$

where Y is gross output, E_i, $i = 1, ..., n$ are n energy inputs, L is labour input, M materials, K capital input, and t denotes a technology index so that we can also define technical change as $\partial f(\cdot)/\partial t$. We assume that the production function (3.1) is homothetically weakly separable in energy, so that it can be written as

$$Y = f\left[E(E_1, ..., E_n), L, M, K, t\right] \tag{3.2}$$

where $E(\cdot)$ is a homothetic aggregator function over the n energy types, $E_1, \cdots, E_n$, representing the total energy measure.

Using the duality theory of cost and production functions, Shephard (1953) showed that the cost function corresponding to the homothetically weakly separable production function in (3.2) is also weakly separable, as follows

$$C = g\left[P_E(P_{E_1}, ..., P_{E_n}), P_L, P_M, P_K, t\right]$$

where $P_E(\cdot)$ is an energy price aggregator function, often interpreted as the price per unit of energy. The energy price aggregator function, $P_E(\cdot)$, can be represented by an arbitrary unit cost function.

In this chapter, we also started with the translog price aggregator function. We followed Ryan and Wales (1998) and Moschini (1999) and, as in Feng and Serletis (2008), treated the curvature property as a maintained hypothesis and built it into the model. The results, however, with the energy data used in this chapter, were disappointing in terms of theoretical regularity violations and inferences about the own-price elasticities and the Allen own elasticities of substitution, invalidating the use of the translog model. These problems with the translog specification led us to use a locally flexible functional form for which the theoretical curvature conditions can be imposed globally. This is the normalized quadratic (NQ) cost function, introduced by Diewert and Wales (1987), to which we now turn. See Diewert and Wales (1987), Diewert and Fox (2009), and also Barnett and Serletis (2008) for more details regarding the NQ form.

The NQ cost function is given by

$$C\left(\boldsymbol{p}, y, t\right) = y\left[\sum_{i=1}^{n}\beta_i p_i + \frac{1}{2}\frac{\sum_{i=1}^{n}\sum_{j=1}^{n}\beta_{ij}p_i p_j}{\sum_{i=1}^{N}\alpha_i p_i} + \sum_{i=1}^{n}\beta_{it}p_i t\right] \quad (3.3)$$

where we impose two restrictions on the $\boldsymbol{B} \equiv [\beta_{ij}]$ matrix, after picking a reference (base-period) vector of normalized prices $\boldsymbol{p}^* \gg \boldsymbol{0}_n$,

$$\beta_{ij} = \beta_{ji}, \quad \text{for all } i, j; \quad (3.4)$$

$$\boldsymbol{Bp}^* = \boldsymbol{0}, \quad \text{for some } \boldsymbol{p}^* > \boldsymbol{0}. \quad (3.5)$$

Restrictions (3.4) and (3.5) ensure the flexibility of the NQ form — see Diewert and Wales (1988) for a formal proof. In addition, the reference price vector $\boldsymbol{p}^*$ in (3.5) is determined in such a way that $\boldsymbol{p}^* = \boldsymbol{1}_n$. Further, the α vector ($\alpha > \boldsymbol{0}$) is usually predetermined. As discussed by Diewert and Fox (2009), the two most frequent a priori choices for the α vector of parameters are a vector of ones ($\alpha = \boldsymbol{1}_n$) or the sample mean of the observed input vectors ($\alpha = (1/T)\sum_{t=1}^{T}\boldsymbol{x}_t$). Here, we used the latter.

To obtain equations that are amenable to estimation, we apply Shephard's (1953) lemma,

$$x_i = \frac{\partial C\left(\boldsymbol{p}, y, t\right)}{\partial p_i}, \quad i = 1, ..., n \quad (3.6)$$

to equation (3.3), and by dividing through by y, we obtain the following input-output equations

$$\frac{x_i}{y} = \beta_i + \sum_{j=1}^{n}\beta_{ij}\frac{p_i}{\sum_{i=1}^{n}\alpha_i p_i}$$

$$-\frac{1}{2}\alpha_i\left(\sum_{i=1}^{n}\sum_{j=1}^{n}\beta_{ij}\frac{p_i}{\sum_{i=1}^{n}\alpha_i p_i}\frac{p_j}{\sum_{j=1}^{n}\alpha_j p_j}\right) + \beta_{it}t. \quad (3.7)$$

Before estimating the system in (3.7), we express the main diagonal elements of the $\boldsymbol{B}$ matrix, β_{ii}, in terms of its off-diagonal elements by using equation (3.5) and assuming that $\boldsymbol{p}^* = \boldsymbol{1}_n$. Thus, by estimating the input-output equations (3.7), we obtain estimates of β_i, the technical change parameters β_{it}, and the off-diagonal elements of the $\boldsymbol{B}$ matrix, β_{ij} $(i \neq j)$. The main diagonal elements of the $\boldsymbol{B}$ matrix can be recovered from the restrictions imposed.

The Hessian matrix of the cost function (3.3) is obtained as follows

$$
\nabla_{p_i p_j} C\left(\boldsymbol{p}, y, t\right) = \frac{\beta_{ij}}{\sum_{i=1}^{n} \alpha_i p_i} - \frac{\alpha_i \left(\sum_{j=1}^{n} \beta_{ij} p_j\right)}{\left(\sum_{i=1}^{n} \alpha_i p_i\right)^2}
$$
$$
- \frac{\alpha_i \left(\sum_{i=1}^{n} \beta_{ij} p_i\right)}{\left(\sum_{i=1}^{n} \alpha_i p_i\right)^2} + \frac{\alpha_i \alpha_j \left(\sum_{i=1}^{n} \sum_{j=1}^{n} p_i \beta_{ij} p_j\right)}{\left(\sum_{i=1}^{n} \alpha_i p_i\right)^3}. \tag{3.8}
$$

Using the restrictions $\sum_{j=1}^{n} \beta_{ij} p_j^* = \boldsymbol{0}_n$ at the reference point, we have $\sum_{i=1}^{n} \sum_{j=1}^{n} p_i^* \beta_{ij} p_j^* = \sum_{i=1}^{n} \left(p_i^* \left(\sum_{j=1}^{n} \beta_{ij} p_j^*\right)\right) = 0$. Thus evaluating the above equation at $(\boldsymbol{p}^*, t^*)$ yields the following equation

$$
\nabla_{p_i p_j} C\left(\boldsymbol{p}, y, t\right) = \frac{\beta_{ij}}{\left(\sum_{i=1}^{n} \alpha_i p_i^*\right)}. \tag{3.9}
$$

Multiplying both sides of (3.9) by y and rearranging, we get $\nabla_{p_i p_j} C\left(\boldsymbol{p}, y, t\right) = \boldsymbol{\alpha}' \ \boldsymbol{p}^{-1} \boldsymbol{B}$. Thus, the negative semidefiniteness of $\nabla_{p_i p_j} C\left(\boldsymbol{p}, y, t\right)$ at the reference point requires that $\boldsymbol{B}$ is negative semidefinite. More importantly, the negative semidefiniteness of $\boldsymbol{B}$ is not only the necessary condition for $\nabla_{p_i p_j} C\left(\boldsymbol{p}, y, t\right)$ to be concave locally at the reference point as we just showed, but it is also a sufficient condition for $\nabla_{p_i p_j} C\left(\boldsymbol{p}, y, t\right)$ to be concave globally (concave at every possible and imaginable point) — see Diewert and Wales (1987) for more details.

In practice, the concavity of $C\left(\boldsymbol{p}, y, t\right)$ may not be satisfied, in the sense that the estimated $\boldsymbol{B}$ matrix may not be negative semidefinite. In this case, to ensure global concavity (concavity at all possible prices) of the NQ cost function, we follow Diewert and Wales (1987) and Feng and Serletis (2008) and impose

$$
\boldsymbol{B} = -\boldsymbol{K}\boldsymbol{K}' \tag{3.10}
$$

where $\boldsymbol{K}$ is a lower triangular matrix which satisfies

$$
\boldsymbol{K}'\boldsymbol{p}^* = \boldsymbol{0}_n. \tag{3.11}
$$

Note that (3.11) and the lower triangular structure of $\boldsymbol{K}$ imply

$$\sum_{i=1}^{n} k_{ij} = 0, \qquad j = 1, ..., n. \tag{3.12}$$

As an example, for the case of three inputs (3.10) and (3.12) imply

$$\beta_{11} = -k_{11}^2 = -(k_{21} + k_{31})^2\,;$$
$$\beta_{12} = -k_{11}k_{21} = (k_{21} + k_{31})\,k_{21};$$
$$\beta_{13} = -k_{11}k_{31} = (k_{21} + k_{31})\,k_{31};$$
$$\beta_{22} = -\left(k_{21}^2 + k_{22}^2\right) = -k_{21}^2 - k_{32}^2;$$
$$\beta_{23} = -\left(k_{21}k_{31} + k_{22}k_{32}\right) = -k_{21}k_{31} + k_{32}^2;$$
$$\beta_{33} = -\left(k_{31}^2 + k_{32}^2 + k_{33}^2\right) = -\left(k_{31}^2 + k_{32}^2\right).$$

That is, we replace the elements of $\boldsymbol{B}$ in the input-output equations (3.7) by the elements of $\boldsymbol{K}$, thus ensuring global curvature. It should be noted that in the case of the NQ cost model, concavity is imposed globally rather than locally at the reference point as in the case of the translog specification. The main advantage of the NQ specification comes from its property that correct curvature conditions can be imposed globally without destroying the flexibility of the functional form.

Finally, even though the NQ model produces results superior to those of the other locally flexible functional forms such as, for example, the translog and generalized Leontief, yet it still has its own limitations. First of all, as a locally flexible form, the NQ often fails to satisfy the conditions of concavity and monotonicity which have to be imposed separately, reducing the flexibility of the model (although not as drastically as in the case of the translog) — on this issue, see Barnett and Serletis (2008). And secondly, the lack of a theoretical framework does not allow extending the model to incorporate, for example, the possibility of lagged responses (dynamic NQ). To our knowledge, most of the theoretical work on the NQ form is limited to papers by Diewert and Wales (1987, 1988) and more recently by Diewert and Fox (2009).

3.3   Econometric Methodology

In order to estimate the equation system (3.7), a stochastic component, ϵ_t, is added to the set of input-output equations as follows

$$\boldsymbol{w}_t = \boldsymbol{\psi}\left(\boldsymbol{p}_t, t, \boldsymbol{\theta}\right) + \boldsymbol{\epsilon}_t \tag{3.13}$$

where $\boldsymbol{w} = (w_1, \cdots, w_n)'$ is the vector of input-output ratios. ϵ_t is a vector of stochastic errors and we assume that $\epsilon \sim N(\boldsymbol{0}, \boldsymbol{\Omega})$ where $\boldsymbol{0}$ is a null matrix and $\boldsymbol{\Omega}$ is the $n \times n$ symmetric positive definite error covariance matrix. $\boldsymbol{\psi}(\boldsymbol{p}_t, t, \boldsymbol{\theta}) = (\psi_1(\boldsymbol{p}_t, t, \boldsymbol{\theta}), \cdots, \psi_n(\boldsymbol{p}_t, t, \boldsymbol{\theta}))'$, and $\psi_i(\boldsymbol{p}_t, t, \boldsymbol{\theta})$ is given by the right-hand side of (3.7). In estimating the model, we proxy y in (3.7) by a Divisia quantity index, obtained by dividing total expenditure on all fuels by the corresponding Divisia price index.

Again, we employ different elasticity measures to investigate the substitutability/complementarity relationship between fuels. The Allen-Uzawa elasicity of substitution between fuels i and j, σ_{ij}^a, can be calculated as

$$\sigma_{ij}^a = \frac{CC_{ij}}{C_i C_j}$$

where C is the cost function in (3.3) and C_i and C_{ij} are the first and second partial derivatives of the cost function with respect to input prices, $C_i = \partial C / \partial p_i$ and $C_{ij} = \partial^2 C / \partial p_i \partial p_j$. See Uzawa (1964) and Diewert (1974) for more details. If $\sigma_{ij}^a > 0$ (that is, if increasing the jth price increases the optimal quantity of fuel i), we say that fuels i and j are Allen-Uzawa (net) substitutes. If $\sigma_{ij}^a < 0$, they are Allen-Uzawa (net) complements.

The own- and cross-price elasticities can be calculated as

$$\eta_{ij} = \frac{C_{ij} p_j}{C_i}.$$

Finally, Blackorby and Russell (1989) show that the Morishima elasticity of substitution between fuels i and j, σ_{ij}^m, can be expressed as

$$\sigma_{ij}^m = \eta_{ij} - \eta_{jj}.$$

Recall that the Morishima elasticity looks at the impact on the ratio of two inputs, x_i / x_j. If $\sigma_{ij}^m > 0$ (that is, if increasing the jth price increases the optimal quantity of fuel i relative to the optimal quantity of fuel j), we say that fuel j is a Morishima (net) substitute for fuel i. If $\sigma_{ij}^m < 0$, fuel j is a Morishima net complement to fuel i.

In this chapter, the estimation is performed in TSP/GiveWin (version 5), using the FIML procedure that delivers results identical to those of the iterative Zellner estimation. The theoretical regularity conditions are checked as discussed in the previous two chapters.

3.4 The International Sectoral Data

For the purpose of our sectoral analysis, we calculate the aggregate quantities of individual fuels for the industrial, residential, electricity generation, and transportation sectors, using *Extended Energy Balances* series published by the International Energy Agency (IEA). All fuel quantities are expressed in kilotonnes of oil equivalent (ktoe). Individual fuel prices, in U.S. dollars per tonne of oil equivalent (toe), come from the *Energy Prices and Taxes* database also provided by the IEA. By definition, these are actually paid (i.e., net of rebates) end-use prices that include all taxes (except VAT) and transporation costs to the consumer.

For most counties, the above mentioned IEA databases provide data on fuel quantities and prices for the period from 1980 to 2006 ($T = 27$). While increasing the number of observations is highly desirable for improving the behavior of econometric models, doing so in our case would involve drawing data from less reliable sources and, more importantly, is decidedly impossible in the case of developing countries for which IEA is the only source of energy statistics. Moreover, while energy consumption data are readily available for almost all sectors across different countries, fuel price data are available for only a small number of sectors. These data limitations make it impossible to deal with all sectors and for all countries, so we estimate models for the mentioned four sectors of those countries for which fuel quantity and price data are available for at least 17 years. In this way, we are left with only 15 countries to carry out the sectoral analysis, with the maximum possible number of observations per country being 27.

For the purpose of providing an international comparison, we divide the selected countries into three groups in accordance with the most recent World Bank's country classification by income. In particular, taking into consideration the fact that a large part of the empirical literature on interfuel substitution pertains to developed economies, our benchmark group consists of six high-income countries: Canada, France, Japan, Italy, the United Kingdom, and the United States; Germany is not included in this group, because of distortions in the quantity data following the unification of the country in the 1990s. The second group includes five upper-middle to high-income economies: Poland, Hungary, Mexico, Turkey, and Venezuela. The third group of countries includes four lower-middle to low-income economies: China, India, South Africa, and Thailand.

Whenever possible, we use a four-input model, consisting either of petroleum products ("oil") (o), natural gas (g), coal (c), and electricity (e). For some sectors, however, we use a three-input model, either because of the structure of the economy (i.e., Turkey did not use natural gas until the 1990s) or because of data availability issues. In particular, for Canada and Venezuela we do not have data for the price of coal and therefore use a three-fuel model consisting of oil, natural gas, and electricity. For China, India, Italy, South Africa, Thailand, and Turkey we do not have data for natural gas prices and thus use a three-fuel model, consisting of oil, coal, and electricity.

For the purpose of our sectoral analysis, we use the high sulphur fuel oil price as the representative price of oil and the steam coal price as the representative price of coal for the industrial sector models. With the residential sector models, we take the light fuel oil price as the representative oil price, and, as in the industrial sector, we use the steam coal price as the representative coal price. For the transportation sector we use the automotive diesel and light fuel oil prices in the industrial sector to proxy the price of diesel and fuel oil in the transportation sector, respectively. Whenever the light fuel oil price is not available (as in the case of Turkey), we consider the industrial high sulphur fuel oil price as the price of fuel oil. We also use the premium leaded gasoline and electricity prices from the household sector to proxy the price of gasoline and electricity, respectively, in the transportation sector. In those cases where the premium leaded gasoline price is unavailable (as, for example, in the case of Canada, Japan, Mexico, and the United States), we use the regular unleaded gasoline price as the price of gasoline.

3.5   Estimation Strategy

Due to a large number of countries (15 countries) and a number of sectors for each country (depending on data availability), we cannot possibly report all of the estimation results. For this reason, in this section we describe our estimation strategy using a representative country and sector — the U.K. industrial sector. Table 3.1 contains a summary of results in terms of parameter estimates and positivity, monotonicity and curvature violations when the NQ model is estimated [that is, equation (3.13)] without the curvature conditions imposed (in the first column) and with the curvature conditions imposed (in the second column). Clearly, although positivity and monotonicity are satisfied at all sample observations, curvature is violated at all sample observations when the curvature conditions

Table 3.1   NQ Parameter Estimates for the U.K. Industrial Sector

Inputs:

1 = oil
2 = natural gas
3 = coal
4 = electricity

Parameter	Unrestricted	Global curvature imposed	Global curvature imposed with AR(1) correction
β_1	.281 (.000)	.269 (.000)	.204 (.000)
β_2	.219 (.000)	.217 (.000)	.221 (.000)
β_3	.047 (.000)	.049 (.000)	.059 (.000)
β_4	.458 (.000)	.469 (.000)	.515 (.000)
β_{12}	.053 (.003)	.046 (.005)	.017 (.083)
β_{13}	−.024 (.000)	−.017 (.003)	−.008 (.055)
β_{14}	−.037 (.004)	.002 (.711)	.008 (.409)
β_{23}	.022 (.005)	.026 (.000)	.018 (.009)
β_{24}	−.010 (.370)	−.004 (.565)	−.009 (.181)
β_{34}	.010 (.132)	.004 (.505)	.005 (.394)
β_{1t}	−.006 (.000)	−.006 (.000)	−.003 (.058)
β_{2t}	−.001 (.045)	−.001 (.092)	−.001 (.232)
β_{3t}	−.001 (.000)	−.001 (.000)	−.002 (.000)
β_{4t}	.007 (.000)	.007 (.000)	.005 (.000)
$\mathrm{Log}L$	377.382	371.933	394.817
Positivity violations	0	0	0
Monotonicity violations	0	0	0
Curvature violations	27	0	0
R_1^2	.85	.76	.92
R_2^2	.36	.35	.74
R_3^2	.87	.82	.95
R_4^2	.93	.88	.96
DW_1	.66	.39	2.73
DW_2	.72	.70	1.52
DW_3	.65	.42	2.20
DW_4	.65	.34	2.01

Note: Sample period, annual data 1980-2006 ($T = 27$).

are not imposed (see the first column of Table 3.1). Because regularity has not been attained, we follow the suggestions of Barnett (2002) and Barnett and Pasupathy (2003) and estimate the NQ model by imposing curvature. In doing so, we impose global curvature, following the procedure suggested by Diewert and Wales (1987).

The results in the second column of Table 3.1 indicate that the imposition of global curvature (at all possible prices), reduces the number of curvature violations to zero, without any induced violations of monotonicity. Table 3.1 also reports the log likelihood values for both the unconstrained and constrained models. By comparing these log likelihood values, we see that the imposition of the curvature constraints does not have much influence on the flexibility of the NQ model. In particular, the log likelihood value decreases only slightly. This means that the constrained NQ model can guarantee inference (including that about the own- and cross-price elasticities as well as the Allen and Morishima elasticities of substitution) consistent with theory, without compromising much of the flexibility of the functional form.

However, as can be seen in the first two columns of Table 3.1, the Durbin-Watson statistics are low, indicating serial correlation in the residuals. Autocorrelation in the disturbances in input-output equations is a common result and has mostly been dealt with by assuming a first-order autoregressive process. We follow this general practice and correct for the serial correlation problem by allowing the possibility of a first-order autoregressive process in the error terms of equation (3.13), as follows

$$\epsilon_t = R\epsilon_{t-1} + u_t$$

where $R = [\rho_{ij}]$ is a matrix of unknown parameters and u_t is a non-autocorrelated vector disturbance term with constant covariance matrix. In this case, estimates of the parameters can be obtained by using a result developed by Berndt and Savin (1975). They showed that if one assumes no autocorrelation across equations (i.e., R is diagonal), the autocorrelation coefficients for each equation must be identical, say ρ. Consequently, by writing equation (3.13) for period $t-1$, multiplying by ρ, and subtracting from (3.13), we can estimate stochastic input-output equations given by

$$w_t = \psi\left(p_t, t, \theta\right) + \rho w_{t-1} - \rho\psi\left(p_{t-1}, t, \theta\right) + u_t. \tag{3.14}$$

We report the parameter estimates in the last column of Table 3.1, using equation (3.14) and with the curvature conditions imposed. It is to be noted that imposing the AR(1) correction seems to complicate the estimation of the system. In particular, the results are sensitive to the initial parameter values. To deal with this problem, we employed a loop-cycle program to go through 10000 sets of initial parameter values and picked the ones that maximize the log-likelihood value.

Next, we use these parameter estimates and report own- and cross-price elasticities, calculated at the mean of the data, in panel A of Table 3.2. Given the nature of our data and the fixed capital stock assumption made earlier, it is clear that the obtained elasticities represent short-run responses rather than long-run behavior. Indeed, as Griffin and Gregory (1976) indicate, intracountry annual time-series fail to capture long-run adjustment of inputs to changes in inputs prices and technology. In contrast, pooled (cross-country) models are not subject to these limitations. See Griffin (1979, p.72) for a detailed discussion regarding this point. Thus, Houthakker (1965) convincingly argues that the individual country (heterogeneous) estimates capture mostly short-run effects, while pooled (homogeneous) estimates reflect mostly long-run adjustments and that the differences between these effects are highly significant both statistically and economically.

As we can see, the investigation of long-run interfuel substitution would involve using pooled international data and, ideally, allowing for dynamic responses within the model. The latter issue was already mentioned in our discussion of the limitations of the NQ model. As for the former, given the scattered nature of international data on sectoral energy prices and consumption, pooling a consistent sectoral cross-country sample does not seem to be a viable option, at least until more inclusive data for the developing countries are available. Both of these adjustments go beyond the scope of the present chapter, however, they do represent fruitful areas of future research (see the next chapter). Moreover, since both homogeneous and heterogeneous estimators have their advantages and drawbacks [see Baltagi and Griffin (1997) for a discussion on the subject], our results provide reliable measures of interfuel substitution — again, keeping in mind that they should be interpreted as short-run effects.

All elasticities reported in this chapter are based on the formulas presented earlier and the p-values have been computed by linearizing the elasticity formulas around the estimated parameter values and then by using the standard formulas for the variance of linear functions of random variables. The own-price elasticities (η_{ii}) in panel A of Table 3.2 are all negative (as predicted by the theory), with the absolute values of these elasticities (in general) being less than 1, which indicates that the demands for all fuels are inelastic. The negativeness of the own-price elasticities theoretically

Table 3.2   Elasticities for the U.K. Industrial Sector

A. Own- and cross-price elasticities

Factor i	η_{io}	η_{ig}	η_{ic}	η_{ie}
o	−.106 (.229)	.113 (.079)	−.050 (.049)	.044 (.480)
g	.082 (.078)	−.130 (.044)	.082 (.007)	−.034 (.336)
c	−.635 (.060)	1.415 (.083)	−1.046 (.155)	.266 (.556)
e	.009 (.484)	−.010 (.330)	.004 (.553)	−.004 (.661)

B. Allen elasticities of substitution

	σ^a_{io}	σ^a_{ig}	σ^a_{ic}	σ^a_{ie}
o	−.823 (.219)	.605 (.079)	−4.669 (.066)	.066 (.480)
g		−.681 (.044)	7.542 (.076)	−.051 (.335)
c			−96.510 (.224)	.401 (.555)
e				−.005 (.662)

C. Morishima elasticities of substitution

	σ^m_{io}	σ^m_{ig}	σ^m_{ic}	σ^m_{ie}
o		.243 (.000)	.995 (.000)	.047 (.444)
g	.189 (.000)		1.128 (.000)	−.030 (.391)
c	−.528 (.116)	1.545 (.058)		.271 (.550)
e	.116 (.000)	.120 (.000)	1.050 (.000)	

Note: Numbers in parentheses are *p*-values.

validates the use of the NQ model.   For the cross-price elasticities (η_{ij}), economic theory does not predict any signs.

From the point of view of energy policy, the measurement of the elasticities of substitution among the different fuels is of prime importance. As already noted, there are currently two methods employed for calculating the partial elasticity of substitution between two variables, the Allen and Morishima.   In panel B of Table 3.2 we show estimates of the Allen elasticities, for the U.K. industrial sector, calculated at the mean of the data. We expect the diagonal terms, representing the Allen own-elasticities of substitution for the different fuels, to be negative.   This expectation is clearly achieved.   Although the diagonal terms in panel B of Table 3.2 are all negative, some of the estimates reported are large (in absolute terms). This can be explained by writing σ_{ij}^a as $\sigma_{ij}^a = \eta_{ij}/s_j$, indicating that σ_{ij}^a is large when the cost share s_j is small.

However, because the Allen elasticity of substitution produces ambiguous results off-diagonal, we use the Morishima elasticity of substitution to investigate the substitutability/complementarity relation between fuels. The asymmetrical Morishima elasticities of substitution — the correct measures of substitution — as documented in panel C of Table 3.1 (Morishima elasticities are also calculated at the mean of the data), are in general less than unity, with only σ_{cg}^m, σ_{gc}^m, and σ_{ec}^m being greater than 1. Moreover, most of the Morishima elasticities of substitution are positive (although small), suggesting substitutability among the different fuels.

3.6 Results

In this section we provide a sectoral investigation, working with a number of countries and sectors for which data are available. In particular, we investigate interfuel substitution in the industrial, residential, electricity generation, and transportation sectors. As discussed above, there are only few papers on sectoral interfuel substitution for comparison of the results. The pioneering works on the subject such as those by Pindyck (1979) and Fuss (1977) are quite outdated by now in terms of used data and, more importantly, fail to deal with theoretical regularity. The latter is also a plague of more recent works — for example, Hall (1986) reports perverse positive own-price elasticities for a number of countries. In this respect, a number of recent papers such as those by Considine (1989), Jones (1995), and Urga and Walters (2003) deliver quite promising results allowing to compare our estimates, if only for the industrial sector of the developed countries.

Data limitations make it impossible to deal with all sectors and for all countries. As noted in the previous section, for the purpose of our sectoral analysis, we do not report parameter estimates, cross-price elasticities, and the Allen elasticities of substitution. We only report the own-price elasticities and the (asymmetrical) Morishima elasticities of substitution, together with p-values, in Tables 3.3-3.13. In fact, the diagonal terms in Tables 3.3-3.13 are the own-price elasticities, η_{ii}, and the off-diagonal ones are the Morishima elasticities of substitution, σ_{ij}^m; note that the cross-price elasticities, η_{ij}, can be calculated using $\eta_{ij} = \sigma_{ij}^m + \eta_{jj}$.

Table 3.3   Own-Price Elasticities and Morishima Elasticities of Substitution in the Industrial Sectors of High-Income Countries

Factor i	Morishima elasticities of substitution			
	σ_{io}^m	σ_{ig}^m	σ_{ic}^m	σ_{ie}^m
Canada				
o	−.107 (.293)	.281 (.001)		−.021 (.819)
g	.175 (.000)	−.136 (.009)		.084 (.089)
c				
e	.101 (.000)	.159 (.000)		−.017 (.460)
France				
o	−.003 (.926)	.042 (.208)	.157 (.000)	.002 (.903)
g	.003 (.750)	−.039 (.309)	.178 (.000)	.021 (.465)
c	.005 (.863)	.325 (.149)	−.157 (.351)	−.128 (.359)
e	.002 (.149)	.045 (.000)	.154 (.000)	−.003 (.666)
Japan				
o	−.142 (.002)	.225 (.000)	.022 (.278)	.016 (.708)
g	.288 (.000)	−.114 (.203)	−.008 (.684)	−.016 (.677)
c	.211 (.030)	.060 (.421)	−.007 (.706)	−.008 (.717)
e	.143 (.000)	.113 (.000)	.007 (.000)	−.002 (.852)
Italy				
o	−.168 (.501)		.034 (.081)	.186 (.440)
g				
c	.545 (.445)		−.024 (.769)	−.324 (.612)
e	.199 (.000)		.022 (.000)	−.029 (.525)
U.K.				
o	−.106 (.229)	.243 (.000)	.995 (.000)	.047 (.444)
g	.189 (.000)	−.130 (.044)	1.128 (.000)	−.030 (.391)
c	−.528 (.116)	1.545 (.058)	−1.046 (.155)	.271 (.550)
e	.115 (.000)	.120 (.000)	1.050 (.000)	−.004 (.661)
U.S.				
o	−.345 (.002)	.261 (.028)	.061 (.082)	.204 (.091)
g	.412 (.000)	−.066 (.311)	.103 (.000)	.011 (.855)
c	.205 (.064)	.194 (.255)	−.093 (.787)	.127 (.748)
e	.369 (.000)	.061 (.005)	.096 (.000)	−.023 (.511)

Notes: Numbers in parentheses are p-values. Diagonal terms are own-price elasticities, η_{ii}; off-diagonal ones are Morishima elasticities of substitution, σ_{ij}^m. The cross-price elasticities, η_{ij}, can be calculated using $\eta_{ij} = \sigma_{ij}^m + \eta_{jj}$.

Reported results are based on equation (3.14) with the curvature conditions imposed. Our results are consistent with neoclassical microeconomic

Table 3.4 Own-Price Elasticities and Morishima Elasticities of Substitution in the Industrial Sectors of Upper-Middle to High-Income Countries

Factor i	Morishima elasticities of substitution			
	σ_{io}^m	σ_{ig}^m	σ_{ic}^m	σ_{ie}^m
Poland				
o	−.244 (.000)	.289 (.000)	−.002 (.970)	.122 (.214)
g	.297 (.000)	−.116 (.003)	.088 (.003)	.023 (.538)
c	.220 (.000)	.205 (.000)	−.040 (.438)	−.015 (.640)
e	.253 (.000)	.120 (.000)	.036 (.000)	−.010 (.445)
Hungary				
o	−.005 (.975)	.000 (.959)		.000 (.992)
g	.000 (.904)	−.000 (.973)		−.000 (.992)
c				
e	.000 (.736)	.000 (.883)		−.000 (.996)
Mexico				
o	−.218 (.256)	.319 (.100)		.115 (.518)
g	.251 (.000)	−.173 (.034)		.184 (.003)
c				
e	.222 (.000)	.212 (.000)		−.042 (.027)
Turkey				
o	−.190 (.094)		−.018 (.814)	.246 (.030)
g				
c	.172 (.007)		−.002 (.899)	.056 (.494)
e	.222 (.000)		.005 (.710)	−.036 (.202)
Venezuela				
o	−.073 (.088)	.087 (.003)		.048 (.333)
g	.088 (.000)	−.050 (.054)		.047 (.079)
c				
e	.077 (.000)	.058 (.000)		−.012 (.118)

Note: See notes to Table 3.3.

theory, as the negativeness of the own-price elasticities and the own Allen elasticities of substitution theoretically validate the use of the NQ model for each country and for each sector. Moreover, the theoretical regularity conditions of positivity, monotonicity, and concavity are also satisfied for each country and for each sector. The statistical significance of the reported results, however, should be interpreted with caution, given the small sample sizes.

3.6.1   *Industrial Sector*

Because of data limitations, we estimated a number of four- and three-fuel
models for the industrial sectors of the countries shown in the following
table

Industrial sector models

4-fuels, (o, g, e, c)	3-fuels, (o, g, e)	3-fuels, (o, c, e)
France	Canada	Italy
Japan	Hungary	South Africa
Poland	Mexico	Thailand
United Kingdom	Venezuela	Turkey
United States		

The sample period is from 1980 to 2006 for all countries ($T = 27$),
except for Poland (1986-2006; $T = 21$), Hungary (1985-2006; $T = 22$),
Venezuela (1981-1999; $T = 19$), and South Africa (1990-2005; $T = 16$).
With the industrial sector models, we use the high sulphur fuel oil price as
the representative price of oil and the steam coal price as the representative
price of coal.

The industrial Morishima elasticities of substitution are reported in Tables 3.3, 3.4, and 3.5 for the high-income countries, the upper-middle to
high-income countries, and the lower-middle to low-income countries, respectively. As can be seen from the reported p-values in Tables 3.3-3.5
(as well as those in Tables 3.6-3.13), most of the Morishima elasticities
of substitution are significant at conventional significance levels providing further support for the inferred conclusions as to the substitutabil-
ity/complementarity relationships among the different fuels.

In general, the industrial Morishima elasticities of substitution are less
than unity in absolute terms, with only σ_{cg}^m, σ_{gc}^m, and σ_{ec}^m for the United
Kingdom being greater than 1, indicating strong substitutability between
natural gas and coal (irrespective of whether the price of gas or coal
changes), strong substitutability between electricity and coal when the price
of coal is changing, but mild substitutability when the price of electricity
is changing. Thailand also shows a high potential of substitution, with
oil being highly substitutable with coal and electricity when the price of
oil changes. In addition, the evidence on interfuel substitution in the industrial sectors of the countries under investigation presents two interesting
findings. There is mild (but in general significant) substitutability between
oil and natural gas, irrespective of whether the price of oil or natural gas

Table 3.5   Own-Price Elasticities and Morishima Elasticities of Substitution in the Industrial Sectors of Lower-Middle to Low-Income Countries

Factor i	Morishima elasticities of substitution			
	σ_{io}^m	σ_{ig}^m	σ_{ic}^m	σ_{ie}^m
South Africa				
o	$-.019(.709)$		$.022(.372)$	$.055(.459)$
g				
c	$-.024(.688)$		$-.040(.518)$	$.102(.313)$
e	$.029(.114)$		$.049(.000)$	$-.018(.494)$
Thailand				
o	$-.439\ (.000)$		$.140\ (.000)$	$.484\ (.000)$
g				
c	$.737\ (.000)$		$-.057\ (.144)$	$-.112\ (.209)$
e	$.597\ (.000)$		$.026\ (.000)$	$-.128\ (.000)$

Note: See notes to Table 3.3.

changes. For example, in Canada, $\sigma_{go}^m = .175$ with a p-value of .000 and $\sigma_{og}^m = .281$ with a p-value of .001; in Japan, $\sigma_{go}^m = .288$ with a p-value of .000 and $\sigma_{og}^m = .225$ with a p-value of .000; and in the United States, $\sigma_{go}^m = .412$ with a p-value of .000 and $\sigma_{og}^m = .261$ with a p-value of .028. Also, there is mild (but again significant) substitutability between electricity and oil when the price of oil changes. In the United States, for example, $\sigma_{eo}^m = .369$ with a p-value of .000; in Italy, $\sigma_{eo}^m = .199$ with a p-value of .000; and in Thailand, $\sigma_{eo}^m = .597$ with a p-value of .000.

Overall, we can see that the industrial sector presents broad evidence of interfuel substitution between energy inputs throughout our international sample. Moreover, developed countries tend to exhibit higher potential of fuel substitution than the developing ones. This fact can be explained by the nature of the industrial sector that consists of all facilities and equipment used for producing, processing, or assembling goods. Nowadays, the interfuel substitution is no rare occasion in the production process, since modern technology allows using any of the studied energy goods as inputs and often interchangeably. Consequently, countries with higher level of technology tend to have less difficulty switching between energy inputs even in the short-run.

Table 3.6 Own-Price Elasticities and Morishima Elasticities of Substitution in the Residential Sectors of High-Income Countries

Factor i	σ_{io}^m	σ_{ig}^m	σ_{ic}^m	σ_{ie}^m
	\multicolumn{4}{c}{Morishima elasticities of substitution}			

Factor i	σ_{io}^m	σ_{ig}^m	σ_{ic}^m	σ_{ie}^m
Canada				
o	−.539 (.039)	.349 (.040)		.287 (.320)
g	.602 (.000)	−.071 (.127)		.034 (.532)
c				
e	.563 (.000)	.073 (.000)		−.027 (.491)
France				
o	−.209 (.002)	.476 (.000)		−.051 (.388)
g	.377 (.000)	−.213 (.012)		.048 (.405)
c				
e	.196 (.000)	.230 (.000)		−.003 (.661)
Japan				
o	−.216 (.327)	−.059 (.844)		.350 (.052)
g	.188 (.006)	−.041 (.743)		.102 (.516)
c				
e	.234 (.000)	.056 (.082)		−.033 (.406)
U.K.				
o	−.027 (.515)	.815 (.010)	.042 (.689)	−.279 (.330)
g	.037 (.000)	−.276 (.000)	.160 (.003)	.380 (.000)
c	−.006 (.894)	1.139 (.236)	−.122 (.633)	−.554 (.416)
e	.020 (.000)	.462 (.000)	.096 (.000)	−.153 (.008)
U.S.				
o	−.339 (.019)	.042 (.782)		.322 (.058)
g	.350 (.000)	−.003 (.985)		.014 (.933)
c				
e	.363 (.000)	.001 (.981)		−.022 (.684)

Note: See notes to Table 3.3.

Comparing the obtained elasticities with those from Jones (1996) and Urga and Walters (2003), our results appear to be generally smaller in magnitude (in absolute values). However, taking into account that in contrast to mentioned long-run findings, our elasticities are short-run responses, small absolute values seem entirely logical — for example, Baltagi and Griffin (1997) find that short-run elasticities are, on average, four times smaller than the corresponding long-run ones. This is what we see happening in our case. For example compare our $\sigma_{oc}^m = .157$ for France with

Table 3.7   Own-Price Elasticities and Morishima Elasticities of Substitution in the Residential Sectors of Upper-Middle to High-Income Countries

Factor i	Morishima elasticities of substitution			
	σ_{io}^m	σ_{ig}^m	σ_{ic}^m	σ_{ie}^m
Poland				
o				
g		−.013 (.606)	.518 (.000)	.065 (.214)
c		.098 (.318)	−.449 (.073)	.484 (.007)
e		−.014 (.570)	.597 (.000)	−.121 (.027)
Hungary				
o	−.020 (.675)	.080 (.280)	.756 (.000)	−.011 (.852)
g	.033 (.137)	−.035 (.494)	.708 (.000)	.083 (.035)
c	.197 (.407)	−.217 (.671)	−.722 (.243)	.843 (.170)
e	.005 (.678)	.062 (.043)	.757 (.000)	−.048 (.177)
Turkey				
o	−.108 (.153)		.095 (.018)	.107 (.047)
g				
c	.291 (.153)		−.060 (.556)	−.088 (.432)
e	.160 (.000)		042 (.001)	−.035 (.292)
Venezuela				
o	−.002 (.962)	.037 (.012)		.002 (.833)
g	.004 (.923)	−.037 (.683)		.035 (.621)
c				
e	−.000 (.944)	.041 (.000)		−.003 (.713)

Note: See notes to Table 3.3.

Jones (1996, p. 819) static elasticity $\sigma_{oc}^m = .63$; for the U.K.: $\sigma_{go}^m = .189$ vs $\sigma_{go}^m = 1.22$; for the U.S.: $\sigma_{oe}^m = .204$ vs $\sigma_{oe}^m = .74$, etc. We find similar relationships comparing our results for the U.S. industrial sector with those of Urga and Walters (2003).

3.6.2   *Residential Sector*

We also estimated a number of four- and three-fuel models for the residential sectors of the countries shown in the following table

Table 3.8   Own-Price Elasticities and Morishima Elasticities of Substitution in the Residential Sectors of Lower-Middle to Low-Income Countries

Factor i	Morishima elasticities of substitution			
	σ_{io}^m	σ_{ig}^m	σ_{ic}^m	σ_{ie}^m
South Africa				
o	−.475 (.116)		.490 (.000)	.266 (.323)
g				
c	1.045 (.002)		−.267 (.318)	.290 (.155)
e	.500 (.000)		.255 (.000)	−.013 (.537)

Note: See notes to Table 3.3.

Table 3.9   Own-Price Elasticities and Morishima Elasticities of Substitution in the Electricity Generation Sectors of High-Income Countries

Factor i	Morishima elasticities of substitution			
	σ_{io}^m	σ_{ig}^m	σ_{ic}^m	σ_{ie}^m
Japan				
o	−.002 (.946)	.035 (.551)	.010 (.749)	
g	.006 (.891)	−.030 (.603)	.040 (.183)	
c	−.000 (.991)	.046 (.018)	−.014 (.539)	
e				
U.K.				
o	−.041 (.926)	−.157 (.889)	.295 (.851)	
g	.038 (.709)	−.043 (.574)	.100 (.179)	
c	.045 (.528)	.092 (.240)	−.054 (.530)	
e				
U.S.				
o	−2.086 (.000)	1.419 (.007)	.937 (.000)	
g	2.186 (.000)	−.155 (.000)	.170 (.000)	
c	2.149 (.000)	.208 (.000)	−.116 (.000)	
e				

Note: See notes to Table 3.3.

Table 3.10 Own-Price Elasticities and Morishima Elasticities of Substitution in the Electricity Generation Sectors of Upper-Middle to High-Income Countries

Factor i	Morishima elasticities of substitution			
	σ_{io}^m	σ_{ig}^m	σ_{ic}^m	σ_{ie}^m
Mexico				
o	−.150 (.081)	.285 (.004)	−.017 (.300)	
g	.216 (.000)	−.087 (.021)	.050 (.000)	
c	.057 (.100)	.209 (.000)	−.029 (.070)	
e				
Turkey				
o	−.657 (.000)	.564 (.001)	.227 (.060)	
g	.803 (.000)	−.105 (.150)	−.012 (.593)	
c	.744 (.000)	.046 (.196)	−.029 (.272)	
e				

Note: See notes to Table 3.3.

Residential sector models			
4-fuels, (o, g, e, c)	3-fuels, (o, g, e)	3-fuels, (o, c, e)	3-fuels, (g, c, e)
United Kingdom	Canada	South Africa	Poland
Hungary	France	Turkey	
	Japan		
	Venezuela		
	United States		

Again, the sample period for the residential sector models is from 1980 to 2006 for all countries $(T = 27)$, except for Venezuela (1981-1999; $T = 19$), Poland (1986-2006; $T = 21$), and South Africa (1990-2005; $T = 16$). With the residential sector models, we use the light fuel oil price as the representative oil price, and, as in the industrial sector, we use the steam coal price as the representative coal price.

As with the industrial Morishima elasticities of substitution, the residential ones, reported in Tables 3.6-3.8, are also mostly statistically significant and generally less than unity with a few exceptions. In particular, there is strong (but statistically insignificant) substitutability between coal and natural gas in the residential sector of the United Kingdom when the price

Table 3.11   Own-Price Elasticities and Morishima Elasticities of Substitution
in the Transportation Sectors of High-Income Countries

Factor i	Morishima elasticities of substitution			
	σ_{io}^m	σ_{ie}^m	σ_{id}^m	σ_{is}^m
Canada				
o	−.611 (.010)	−.163 (.220)	.436 (.073)	.547 (.153)
e	.324 (.040)	−.145 (.131)	.230 (.061)	.264 (.192)
d	.625 (.000)	.152 (.000)	−.044 (.227)	.040 (.284)
s	.618 (.000)	.148 (.000)	.052 (.000)	−.019 (.261)
France				
o				
e		−.001 (.887)	.083 (.426)	.246 (.022)
d		−.001 (.836)	−.112 (.002)	.331 (.000)
s		.004 (.752)	.325 (.000)	−.216 (.004)
Japan				
o	−.010 (.634)	.348 (.008)	.395 (.040)	.011 (.885)
e	−.024 (.499)	−.469 (.048)	.700 (.003)	.079 (.776)
d	.018 (.051)	.550 (.000)	−.225 (.016)	.186 (.009)
s	.010 (.000)	.471 (.000)	.274 (.000)	−.050 (.064)
Italy				
o				
e		−.005 (.869)	−.014 (.808)	.050 (.553)
d		.003 (.575)	−.012 (.799)	.033 (.498)
s		.007 (.299)	.028 (.592)	−.019 (.721)
U.K.				
o	−.201 (.342)	.425 (.307)	−1.170 (.363)	1.250 (.409)
e	.215 (.000)	−.227 (.341)	−.045 (.928)	.334 (.594)
d	.196 (.000)	.223 (.000)	−.035 (.635)	.085 (.339)
s	.204 (.000)	.237 (.000)	.064 (.272)	−.042 (.566)
U.S.				
o	−2.041 (.785)	7.090 (.765)	14.517 (.819)	−23.523 (.800)
e	−2.074 (.819)	−.115 (.430)	−.234 (.450)	.392 (.334)
d	−2.041 (.822)	.112 (.000)	−.005 (.705)	.012 (.446)
s	−2.040 (.823)	.116 (.000)	.008 (.183)	−.005 (.521)

Note: See notes to Table 3.3.

of natural gas changes ($\sigma_{cg}^m = 1.139$ with a *p*-value of .236). There is
also strong (and statistically significant) substitutability between coal and
oil in the residential sector of South Africa when the price of oil changes
($\sigma_{co}^m = 1.045$ with a *p*-value of .002). In general, there is evidence of
mild substitutability between oil and natural gas (irrespective of whether

Table 3.12   Own-Price Elasticities and Morishima Elasticities of Substitution in the Transportation Sectors of Upper-Middle to High-Income Countries

| Factor i | Morishima elasticities of substitution | | | |
	σ_{io}^m	σ_{ie}^m	σ_{id}^m	σ_{is}^m
Mexico				
o				
e		−.251 (.001)	.484 (.000)	−.215 (.031)
d		.260 (.000)	−.016 (.013)	.008 (.142)
s		.250 (.000)	.018 (.000)	−.001 (.369)
Turkey				
o	−.079 (.806)	−.032 (.840)	.240 (.779)	−.117 (.837)
e	.063 (.250)	−.008 (.862)	.051 (.800)	−.022 (.858)
d	.080 (.000)	.008 (.000)	−.003 (.829)	.003 (.753)
s	.077 (.000)	.007 (.003)	.006 (.761)	−.002 (.907)

Note: See notes to Table 3.3.

Table 3.13   Own-Price Elasticities and Morishima Elasticities of Substitution in the Transportation Sectors of Lower-Middle to Low-Income Countries

| Factor i | Morishima elasticities of substitution | | | |
	σ_{io}^m	σ_{ie}^m	σ_{id}^m	σ_{is}^m
Indonesia				
o				
e		−.145 (.487)	−.302 (.391)	.515 (.051)
d		.141 (.008)	−.043 (.230)	.071 (.035)
s		.148 (.002)	.064 (.000)	−.024 (.106)
South Africa				
o				
e		−.213 (.027)	−.182 (.277)	.446 (.064)
d		.196 (.000)	−.015 (.490)	.068 (.061)
s		.231 (.000)	.032 (.091)	−.036 (.220)

Note: See notes to Table 3.3.

the price of oil or the price of gas changes).   For example, in Canada, $\sigma_{go}^m = .602$ with a p-value of .000 and $\sigma_{og}^m = .349$ with a p-value of .040; in France, $\sigma_{go}^m = .377$ with a p-value of .000 and $\sigma_{og}^m = .476$ with a p-value of .000; and in the United Kingdom, $\sigma_{go}^m = .037$ with a p-value of .000 and

$\sigma_{og}^m = .815$ with a p-value of .010. There is also mild (but statistically significant) substitutability between electricity and oil, when the price of oil is changing, in the residential sectors of Canada ($\sigma_{eo}^m = .563$ with a p-value of .000), France ($\sigma_{eo}^m = .196$ with a p-value of .000), Japan ($\sigma_{eo}^m = .234$ with a p-value of .000), the United States ($\sigma_{eo}^m = .363$ with a p-value of .000), Turkey ($\sigma_{eo}^m = .160$ with a p-value of .000), and South Africa ($\sigma_{eo}^m = .500$ with a p-value of .000).

Our evidence on interfuel substitution in the residential sector fails to detect any distinctive pattern regarding either the substitution between any particular fuels or the relationship between interfuel substitution and the level of economic development. This conclusion is quite expected. Keeping in mind that energy inputs in the residential sector are used primarily for heating, it seems natural that interfuel substitution in that sector is only a function of country's economic structure, its geographical location, and the available natural resources. For example, Poland and Hungary show mild substitutability between coal and other fuels in their residential sectors. This can be explained by the fact that coal is the most abundant energy resource in those two countries, and has been successfully competing with other fuels used in residential heating plants.

3.6.3 *Electricity Generation Sector*

For the electricity generation sector we are estimating only three-fuel (o, g, c) models for the five countries shown in the following table

Electricity-generation sector models

3-fuels, (o, g, c)
Japan
United Kingdom
United States
Mexico
Turkey

The sample period for the electricity-generation sector models is from 1980 to 2006 for the United States, the United Kingdom, and Mexico ($T = 27$), from 1980 to 1997 for Japan ($T = 18$), and from 1988 to 2006 for Turkey ($T = 19$). The results are presented in Tables 3.9-3.11.

As Tables 3.9-3.10 reveal, the short-run Morishima elasticities of substitution in the electricity generation sector are in general statistically significant and also less than unity. Only σ_{go}^m, σ_{co}^m, and σ_{og}^m for the United States are greater than 1 in absolute terms. In fact, $\sigma_{go}^m = 2.186$ with a p-value of .000 and $\sigma_{og}^m = 1.419$ with a p-value of .007, suggesting that oil and natural gas are Morishima substitutes irrespective of whether the price of oil or the price of gas is changing. Also, $\sigma_{co}^m = 2.149$ with a p-value of .000 and $\sigma_{oc}^m = .937$ with a p-value of .000, suggesting that oil and coal are also Morishima substitutes irrespective of whether the price of oil or the price of coal changes. These elasticities are highly statistically significant.

The results for the United States, particularly the high oil-gas substitution, can be explained by the high share of dual and multi-fired plants in that country, since the most common substitution possibility in these is between gas and oil. This evidence is also consistent with Söderholm (2000) who reports notable short-run substitution between oil and gas in Western Europe, using models different than ours. In this regard, the scope for interfuel substitution is likely to be higher in the United States than in western European countries, given the greater extent of plants able to switch gas and oil in the United States. There is also significant evidence of substitutability in Turkey between oil and gas, irrespective of which price changes, as $\sigma_{go}^m = .803$ with a p-value of .000 and $\sigma_{og}^m = .564$ with a p-value of .001. Also, in Turkey there is evidence of mild substitutability between coal and oil, irrespective of whether the price of oil or the price of coal changes.

The evidence regarding interfuel substitution in the electricity generation sector is similar to that for the industrial and residential sectors, revealing no distinct patterns as to particular fuels or country groups. However, the number of countries used to investigate interfuel substitution in the electricity generation sector is too limited to reach any conclusions regarding its relevance in the government decision-making process. Only in the case of the United States we find convincing evidence of substitutability among fossil fuels, suggesting that efforts by U.S. policymakers to substitute coal with more environmentally friendly sources of energy seem to have a very solid ground.

3.6.4 *Transportation Sector*

Finally, we estimate a number of four- and three-fuel models for the following fuels (note the different notation in this subsection): fuel oil (o), electricity (e), diesel (d), and gasoline (s). In doing so, because of data limitations, we use the automotive diesel and light fuel oil prices in the industrial sector to proxy the price of diesel and fuel oil, respectively, in the transportation sector. Whenever the light fuel oil price is not available (as in the case of Turkey), we use the industrial high sulphur fuel oil price as the price of fuel oil. We also use the premium leaded gasoline and electricity prices from the household sector to proxy the price of gasoline and electricity, respectively, in the transportation sector. In those cases that the premium leaded gasoline price is missing (as, for example, in the case of Canada, Japan, Mexico, and the United States), we use the regular unleaded gasoline price as the price of gasoline.

Taking into account the specifics of each economy and data limitations, we restrict our analysis to the countries and models shown in the following table

Transportation sector models

4-fuels, (o,d,s,e)	3-fuels, (d,s,e)	3-fuels, (o,s,d)
Canada	France	Indonesia
Japan	Italy	
Turkey	Mexico	
United Kingdom	South Africa	
United States		

The sample period for the transportation sector models is from 1980 to 2006 for Canada, France, Japan, Italy, Mexico, South Africa, Turkey, and the United States ($T = 27$) and from 1980 to 2004 for the United Kingdom and Indonesia ($T = 25$).

The transportation sector Morishima elasticities of substitution are reported in Tables 3.11-3.13. As in the other sectors, these elasticities of substitution are in general statistically significant and less than unity. There are a few exceptions to this rule, such as $\sigma_{od}^m = -1.170$ (with a p-value of .363) and $\sigma_{os}^m = 1.250$ (with a p-value of .409) for the United Kingdom and $\sigma_{oe}^m = 7.090$ (with a p-value of .765), $\sigma_{od}^m = 14.517$ (with a p-value of .819), $\sigma_{os}^m = -23.523$ (with a p-value of .800), $\sigma_{eo}^m = -2.074$ (with a p-value of .819), $\sigma_{do}^m = -2.041$ (with a p-value of .822), and $\sigma_{so}^m = -2.040$ (with a p-value of .823) for the United States. However, as can be seen from the corresponding p-values, none of the large elasticities are statistically significant, and therefore, should be treated with caution. In fact, taking into account the fact that Morishima elasticities of substitution look at the ratio of two inputs, the large values above may reflect the fact that some of the fuels have comparatively small share in the transport sector overall energy consumption rather than indicate strong substitutability relationships.

Overall, we can see that the short-run interfuel substitution is very limited in the transportation sector. At best, we can observe some mild substitution (subject to the correct direction of price changes) between gasoline and diesel in Canada, France, and Japan and between fuel oil and diesel in Canada and Japan. We find electricity and diesel to be mild substitutes in Japan (irrespective of which price changes) and Mexico (when the price of diesel changes). Electricity and gasoline are also mild substitutes in South Africa given the change in the price of gasoline. This finding may be explained by the fact that the transportation sector, as defined by the IEA, includes all vehicles such as cars, boats, trains, planes, etc. Our guess is that the prime use of electricity in this sector is to run trains and subways, and therefore substitution between electricity and other fuels may reflect the fact that consumers tend to switch between different means of transportation, given enough price incentive, like taking a subway to work rather than driving a car.

In addition, the transportation sector exhibits similar patterns to the industrial sector in the sense that on average, rich countries exhibit higher potential of substitution among energy goods than poor countries. In practical terms, and from a policy perspective, programs designed to switch to "greener" fuels will be most feasible in countries like Canada, Japan, the United Kingdom, and the United States.

3.7 Summary and Conclusions

We have investigated interfuel substitution, substitution between petroleum products, natural gas, coal, and electricity, taking a flexible functional form approach and using state-of-the-art recent advances in microeconometrics. In particular, to minimize the potential problem of using a misspecified functional form, we have employed a well-known flexible functional form, the locally flexible normalized quadratic (NQ), introduced by Diewert and Wales (1987). Moreover, motivated by the widespread practice of ignoring the theoretical regularity conditions, we have estimated the model subject to theoretical regularity using methods developed by Diewert and Wales (1987). We have produced inference about the demand for fuels, including in particular that about the Morishima elasticities of substitution, which is consistent with neoclassical microeconomic theory.

Our evidence indicates that the interfuel Morishima elasticities of substitution are (in general) consistently below unity, revealing the limited ability to substitute one source of energy with another. This is consistent with the short-run interpretation of our results and corresponds to findings of other works that investigate sectoral interfuel substitution such as Jones (1996) and Urga and Walters (2003). Moreover, none of the counter-intuitive negative elasticities suggesting complementarity are statistically significant, providing further support to our conclusions.

On average, industrial and residential sectors tend to exhibit higher potential for substitution between energy inputs as compared to the electricity generation and transportation sectors in all three groups of countries. This could be because the majority of the countries in our sample are in various stages of development and do not boast many dual- or multi-fuel electricity generation plants. Söderholm (2000) finds the direct positive correlation between the number of multi-fuel plants and the potential of interfuel substitution in the electricity generation sector. High elasticity values for the electricity generation sector in the United States support this point. Overall, interfuel substitution seems to depend on the structure of the economy, but to be independent of the level of economic development. Hence, policymakers' efforts are more likely to deliver expected results if they are focused on a particular sector or industry rather than on the economy in general.

In addition, we find that developed countries demonstrate higher potential for interfuel substitution in their industrial and transportation sectors as compared to the developing economies. This may suggest that technology plays an important role in defining the possibility of substitution between various energy goods as countries with higher level of technology tend to have less difficulty switching between energy inputs even in the short-run.

Overall, our results highlight the fact that the substitution between different energy inputs has been quite restricted, suggesting that fossil fuels will continue to maintain their major role as a source of energy in the near future. Therefore, such daunting tasks as curbing carbon emissions and preventing climate change require a more active and focused energy policy. Also, because interfuel substitution is limited in the near term, there will be a greater need for relative price changes to induce switching to a lower carbon economy.

Finally, it should be mentioned that although this chapter presents international evidence on interfuel substitution consistent with the theoretical regularity conditions of neoclassical microeconomic theory, in doing so, it uses a locally flexible functional form, as most of the existing empirical energy demand literature does. An innovation in this respect is the use of semi-nonparametric flexible functional forms that possess global flexibility and in which asymptotic inferences are potentially free from any specification error. Two such semi-nonparametric functions are the Fourier flexible functional form, introduced by Gallant (1981), and the Asymptotically Ideal Model (AIM), employed and explained in Barnett and Yue (1988). These models have been recently employed by Serletis and Shahmoradi (2008) in the context of interfuel substitution in U.S. energy demand. Although these semi-nonparametric functions are parameter intensive, their use in the investigation of interfuel substitution and energy demand is a potentially productive area for future research.

Chapter 4

Short- and Long-Run Aggregate Interfuel Substitution*

4.1 Introduction

In this chapter, we build on the work of the previous two chapters and investigate short- and long-run interfuel substitution, using the most recent international data, published by the International Energy Agency (IEA). We also minimize the potential problem of using a misspecified functional form by using the normalized quadratic (NQ) cost function explained in detail in the previous chapter. We estimate the model subject to global curvature and provide inference, and also a policy perspective, using parameter estimates that are consistent with all three theoretical regularity conditions of neoclassical microeconomic theory (positivity, monotonicity, and curvature).

The chapter is organized as follows. Section 4.2 discusses estimation issues while Section 4.3 discusses the data. Section 4.4 estimates the model using time series data for each country, assesses the results in terms of their consistency with optimizing behavior, and explores the economic significance of the results. The final section concludes the chapter.

4.2 Estimation of the NQ System

As noted in the previous chapter, most of the empirical energy demand literature has used the translog flexible functional form, due to Christensen *et al.* (1975). See, for example, Berndt and Wood (1975), Fuss (1977), Pindyck (1979), Uri (1979), Considine (1989), Hall (1986), and Jones (1996), among

*This article was published in *Energy Economics*, Vol 33, Serletis, Apostolos, Govinda Timilsina, and Olexandr Vasetsky, "International Evidence on Aggregate Short-Run and Long-Run Interfuel Substitution," 209-216. Copyright Elsevier (2011).

others. However, Guilkey *et al.* (1983) show that the translog is globally
regular if and only if technology is Cobb-Douglas. In other words, the
translog performs well if substitution between all factors is close to unity.
They also show that the regularity properties of the translog model deteriorate rapidly when substitution diverges from unity.

Because of these problems with the translog specification, in this chapter
we follow our work in the previous chapter and use the normalized quadratic
(NQ) cost function. Again, in order to estimate the NQ input-output
equations [see equation (3.7) of Chapter 3], a stochastic component, ϵ_t, is
added to the set of input-output equations as follows

$$w_t = \psi\left(z_t, t, \theta\right) + \epsilon_t \tag{4.1}$$

where $w = (w_1, \cdots, w_n)'$ is the vector of input-output ratios, $z = (z_1, \cdots, z_n)'$ is the vector of the $p_j / \sum_{j=1}^{n} \alpha_j p_j$ ratios, and θ is the vector
of parameters. ϵ_t is a vector of stochastic errors and we assume that $\epsilon \sim N\left(0, \Omega\right)$ where 0 is a null matrix and Ω is the $n \times n$ symmetric positive definite error covariance matrix. $\psi(z_t, t, \theta) = (\psi_1\left(z_t, t, \theta\right), \cdots, \psi_n\left(z_t, t, \theta\right))'$,
and $\psi_i\left(z_t, t, \theta\right)$ is given by the right-hand side of equation (3.7) of Chapter
3.

To distinguish between the long-run and short-run responses, the system in equation (3.7) of Chapter 3 has to be estimated as a pooled set of
cross-sectional and time-series data. Nowadays it has become a standard
practice to interpret the results from the individual country (time-series)
models as capturing mostly short-run effects, while pooled estimates are
treated as reflecting mainly long-run adjustments. The differences between these effects are found to be highly significant both statistically and
economically. Seminal works by Houthakker (1965), Griffin and Gregory
(1976), and Griffin (1979) provide the detailed reasoning behind this argument.

Introducing the respective vectors of coefficients, $\beta = (\beta_1, \cdots, \beta_n)'$, $\gamma = (\beta_{1t}, \cdots, \beta_{nt})'$, and $B \equiv [\beta_{ij}]$ as before, (4.1) can be written as

$$w_{kt} = \beta + B z_{kt} + \gamma t + \epsilon_{kt} \tag{4.2}$$

for $k = 1, \cdots, N$ and $t = 1, \cdots, T$, with k denoting countries and t time.
Estimating equation (3.7) of Chapter 3 in the context of (4.2) proved to
be too restrictive in terms of high standard errors, so following Pindyck
(1979) we let the first order coefficients (β) to vary across countries by
using the country-specific intercept dummy variables, which is equivalent
to estimating the fixed effects model

$$w_{kt} = \sum_{k=1}^{n} \beta_k + B z_{kt} + \gamma t + \epsilon_{kt} \qquad (4.3)$$

for $k = 1, \cdots, N$ and $t = 1, \cdots, T$. Griffin (1979) raised some valid points whether the results from the fixed effect or 'within' models can be interpreted as long-run, and gave preference to the 'between' models for this purpose. However, later works questioned the validity of this argument due to a possible omitted variables problem. See, for example, Baltagi (1995, section 10.6.2). In our case, data limitations make the use of the between estimators impossible and we estimate system (4.3) instead.

Finally, allowing both first (β) and second-order coefficients (B and γ) to vary as in

$$w_{kt} = \sum_{k=1}^{n} \beta_k + \sum_{k=1}^{n} B_k z_{kt} + \sum_{k=1}^{n} \gamma_k t + \epsilon_{kt} \qquad (4.4)$$

for $k = 1, \cdots, N$ and $t = 1, \cdots, T$, is equivalent to estimating separate (time-series) models for each country. We use (4.4) for calculating the short-run elasticities of substitution between different fuels.

Finally, it should be noted that we ignore econometric regularity issues, as we did in the previous two chapters. In this regard, as noted by Feng and Serletis (2008), for input-output demand equations to make sense the variables must be cointegrated in levels; that is, the equation errors must be stationary. However, unit root test results on the residuals of input-output demand equations typically indicate that they are nonstationary, suggesting that some important nonstationary variables might have been omitted. Allowing for first order serial correlation, as is usually done in the literature and in the previous chapter, is almost the same as taking first differences of the data if the autocorrelation coefficient is close to unity. In that case, the equation errors become stationary, but there is no theory for the models in first differences. It is also to be noted that even if the errors are stationary and the estimates are super consistent, as argued by Attfield (1997) and Ng (1995), standard estimation procedures are inadequate for obtaining correctly estimated standard errors for coefficients in cointegrating equations. In that case, if the equations were all linear, the DOLS method of Stock and Watson (1993) or the FM-OLS method of Phillips (1995) could have been used to obtain correctly estimated standard errors. With our nonlinear model, however, some sort of modification of these procedures is called for, but this is a very difficult issue to deal with. For these reasons, in this chapter we ignore econometric regularity issues and only pay attention to economic regularity, as in the previous chapter.

4.3   The International Aggregate Data

Energy consumption data are readily available for almost all countries, but fuel price data are available for only a small number of countries. Because of this data availability problem, we estimate models for those countries for which fuel quantity and price data are available for at least 15 years. For the purpose of providing an international comparison, we use data for three groups of countries, as in the previous chapter: high-income countries, upper-middle to high-income countries, and lower-middle to low-income countries.

Individual fuel (total final) consumption data come from the *World Energy Statistics and Balances,* published by the International Energy Agency (IEA). All fuel quantities are expressed in kilotonnes of oil equivalent (ktoe). Individual fuel prices, in U.S. dollars per tonne of oil equivalent (toe), come from *Energy Prices and Taxes,* also published by the IEA. For consistency across the different countries, we use industrial sector prices as the representative fuel prices. Moreover, we use the high-sulphur fuel oil price as the representative price of oil and the steam coal price as the representative coal price. For those countries for which industrial sector prices are not available, we use different proxies; for example, we use the electricity-generation sector prices as a proxy for the coal price for South Africa and the industrial price of automotive diesel as a proxy for the oil price in Thailand.

Whenever possible, as in the previous chapter, we use a four-input model, consisting of petroleum products ('oil'), natural gas, coal, and electricity. For some countries, however, we use a three-input model, either because of the structure of the economy (i.e., Turkey did not use natural gas until the 1990s) or because of data availability issues. In particular, for Canada and Venezuela, we do not have data for the price of coal and therefore use a three-fuel model consisting of oil, natural gas, and electricity. For China, India, Italy, Thailand, and Turkey we do not have data for natural gas prices and thus use a three-fuel model, consisting of oil, coal, and electricity.

Finally, for the high-income countries (Canada, France, Japan, Italy, the United Kingdom, and the United States) and Mexico, Hungary, Thailand, and Turkey, the sample period is from 1980 to 2006, a total of 27 observations ($T = 27$). For India the sample period is from 1981 to 2005 ($T = 25$), for Venezuela from 1981 to 1999 ($T = 19$), for South Africa from 1980 to 2005 ($T = 26$), for Poland from 1986 to 2006 ($T = 21$), and for China from 1990 to 2006 ($T = 17$).

4.4 Empirical Evidence

4.4.1 *Short-Run Estimates*

First, we start by reporting the results for the individual (short-run) time-series models as represented by system (4.4). Tables 4.1-4.15 contain a summary of results in terms of parameter estimates and positivity, monotonicity, and concavity violations when the NQ model is estimated without the concavity conditions imposed (in the first column) and with the concavity conditions imposed (in the second column). Clearly, although positivity and monotonicity are satisfied at all sample observations, curvature is violated at all sample observations when the curvature conditions are not imposed (see the first column of Tables 4.1-4.15). Because regularity has not been attained, except for Venezuela, we follow the suggestions of Barnett (2002) and Barnett and Pasupathy (2003) and estimate the NQ model for each country by imposing curvature. In doing so, we impose global curvature, following the procedure suggested by Diewert and Wales (1987).

The results in the second column of Tables 4.1-4.15 are impressive, as they indicate that the imposition of global curvature (at all possible prices), reduces the number of curvature violations to zero, without any induced violations of monotonicity; only in the case of Thailand the imposition of curvature produces a monotonicity violation at one data point. Tables 4.1-4.15 also report the log likelihood values for both the unconstrained and constrained models. By comparing these log likelihood values, we see that the imposition of the curvature constraints has not much influence on the flexibility of the NQ model. In particular, the log likelihood values in most cases decrease only slightly. This means that the constrained NQ model can guarantee inference (including that about the own- and cross-price elasticities as well as the Allen and Morishima elasticities of substitution) consistent with theory, without compromising much of the flexibility of the functional form.

We start by reporting the short-run price elasticities in Tables 4.16-4.18 for the six high-income countries (Canada, France, Japan, Italy, the United Kingdom, and the United States), the five upper-middle to high-income countries (Poland, Hungary, Mexico, Turkey, and Venezuela), and the four lower-middle to low-income countries (China, India, South Africa, and Thailand), respectively. All elasticities reported in this chapter are calculated at the mean of the data and the p-values have been computed by linearizing the elasticity formulas around the estimated parameter values and then by using the standard formulas for the variance of linear functions of random variables. The own-price elasticities (η_{ii}) are all negative (as predicted by the theory), with the absolute values of these elasticities (in general) being less than 1, which indicates that the demands for all fuels are inelastic in the short run. Thailand presents the only exception with own-price elasticity for coal, η_{cc}, being -1.120; we will return to this interesting finding later. The negativeness of the own-price elasticities again theoretically validates the use of the NQ model. Moreover, as can be seen from the p-values, most of the elasticities are significant at conventional significance levels providing further support for the inferred conclusions as to the substitutability/complementarity relationships among the different fuels.

Table 4.1   NQ Parameter Estimates for Canada

Inputs:

1 = oil
2 = electricity
3 = natural gas

Parameter	Unrestricted	Global curvature imposed
β_1	.4256 (.000)	.4229 (.000)
β_2	.4087 (.000)	.4103 (.000)
β_3	.1724 (.000)	.1726 (.000)
β_{12}	$-.0174$ (.001)	$-.0048$ (.001)
β_{13}	.0180 (.001)	.0208 (.001)
β_{23}	.0075 (.015)	.0063 (.022)
β_{1t}	$-.0014$ (.008)	$-.0014$ (.001)
β_{2t}	.0016 (.001)	.0016 (.000)
β_{3t}	.0001 (.231)	.0001 (.148)
$\mathrm{Log}L$	301.575	298.689
Positivity violations	0	0
Monotonicity violations	0	0
Curvature violations	27	0
R_1^2	.43	.27
R_2^2	.42	.29
R_3^2	.51	.48

Note: Sample period, annual data 1980-2006 ($T = 27$).

Table 4.2   NQ Parameter Estimates for France

Inputs:

1 = oil
2 = natural gas
3 = coal
4 = electricity

Parameter	Unrestricted	Global curvature imposed
β_1	.5010 (.000)	.4980 (.000)
β_2	.3508 (.000)	.3531 (.000)
β_3	.1336 (.000)	.1335 (.000)
β_4	.0264 (.000)	.0268 (.000)
β_{12}	−.0177 (.000)	−.0012 (.568)
β_{13}	.0108 (.256)	.0104 (.140)
β_{14}	.0014 (.382)	.0009 (.381)
β_{23}	.0022 (.569)	.0012 (.628)
β_{24}	−.0024 (.001)	.0001 (.475)
β_{34}	−.0013 (.523)	−.0009 (.308)
β_{1t}	−.0054 (.000)	−.0053 (.000)
β_{2t}	.0047 (.000)	.0047 (.000)
β_{3t}	.0010 (.000)	.0009 (.000)
β_{4t}	−.0007 (.000)	−.0007 (.000)
Log$L$	481.021	464.366
Positivity violations	0	0
Monotonicity violations	0	0
Curvature violations	27	0
R_1^2	.94	.91
R_2^2	.92	.88
R_3^2	.70	.70
R_4^2	.96	.95

Note: Sample period, annual data 1980-2006 ($T = 27$).

From the point of view of energy policy, the measurement of the elasticities of substitution among the different fuels is of prime importance. As already noted, there are currently two methods employed for calculating the partial elasticity of substitution between two variables, the Allen and Morishima. Tables 4.19-4.21 show estimates of the Allen elasticities. We expect the diagonal terms, representing the Allen own-elasticities of substitution for the different fuels to be negative. This expectation is clearly

Table 4.3   NQ Parameter Estimates for Japan

Inputs:

$1 = $ oil
$2 = $ natural gas
$3 = $ coal
$4 = $ electricity

Parameter	Unrestricted	Global curvature imposed
β_1	.4480 (.000)	.4446 (.000)
β_2	.4780 (.000)	.4804 (.000)
β_3	.0517 (.000)	.0516 (.000)
β_4	.0251 (.000)	.0254 (.000)
β_{12}	−.0010 (.693)	−.0003 (.835)
β_{13}	.0086 (.016)	.0163 (.000)
β_{14}	−.0009 (.807)	.0019 (.338)
β_{23}	−.0108 (.000)	.0003 (.837)
β_{24}	−.0019 (.370)	.0000 (.843)
β_{34}	−.0010 (.746)	−.0018 (.297)
β_{1t}	−.0035 (.000)	−.0034 (.000)
β_{2t}	.0010 (.000)	.0012 (.000)
β_{3t}	.0013 (.000)	.0011 (.000)
β_{4t}	−.0001 (.057)	−.0002 (.000)
Log$L$	514.348	505.482
Positivity violations	0	0
Monotonicity violations	0	0
Curvature violations	27	0
R_1^2	.97	.96
R_2^2	.83	.97
R_3^2	.97	.56
R_4^2	.55	.80

Note: Sample period, annual data 1980-2006 ($T = 27$).

achieved, even though some of the elasticities do not appear to be significant. Although the diagonal terms in Tables 4.19-4.21 are all negative, some of the estimates reported in Tables 4.19-4.21 are disproportionately large (in absolute terms). This is, for example, the case of coal in the United Kingdom and the United States (see Table 4.19) and Hungary and Mexico (see Table 4.20) and also the case of gas in South Africa and coal in Thailand (see Table 4.21). This can be explained by writing σ_{ij}^a as

Table 4.4 NQ Parameter Estimates for Italy

Inputs:

1 = oil
2 = electricity
3 = coal

Parameter	Unrestricted	Global curvature imposed
β_1	.6842 (.000)	.6842 (.000)
β_2	.2990 (.000)	.2988 (.000)
β_3	.0093 (.000)	.0095 (.000)
β_{12}	.0287 (.000)	.0233 (.000)
β_{13}	−.0057 (.005)	−.0020 (.026)
β_{23}	.0006 (.861)	.0022 (.039)
β_{1t}	−.0045 (.074)	−.0045 (.074)
β_{2t}	.0060 (.000)	.0060 (.000)
β_{3t}	−.0001 (.010)	−.0001 (.000)
LogL	386.189	384.920
Positivity violations	0	0
Monotonicity violations	0	0
Curvature violations	27	0
R_1^2	.98	.98
R_2^2	.99	.99
R_3^2	.77	.78

Note: Sample period, annual data 1980-2006 ($T = 27$).

$\sigma_{ij}^a = \eta_{ij}/s_j$, indicating that σ_{ij}^a is large when the cost share s_j is small. However, because the Allen elasticity of substitution produces ambiguous results off-diagonal, we use the Morishima elasticity of substitution to investigate the substitutability/complementarity relation between fuels. The asymmetrical Morishima elasticities of substitution — the correct measures of substitution — as documented in Tables 4.22-4.24 (again Morishima elasticities are reported at the mean of the data), are in general less than unity, with only σ_{oc}^m, σ_{co}^m, σ_{ce}^m, and σ_{ec}^m for Thailand being greater than 1 in absolute terms. Moreover, most of the Morishima elasticities of substitution are positive (although small) and significant, suggesting substitutability among the different fuels.

Table 4.5   NQ Parameter Estimates for U.K.

Inputs:

1 = oil
2 = natural gas
3 = coal
4 = electricity

Parameter	Unrestricted	Global curvature imposed
β_1	.4709 (.000)	.4702 (.000)
β_2	.3266 (.000)	.3259 (.000)
β_3	.1582 (.000)	.1587 (.000)
β_4	.0473 (.000)	.0482 (.000)
β_{12}	.0103 (.001)	.0081 (.029)
β_{13}	.0126 (.016)	.0148 (.000)
β_{14}	$-.0077$ (.006)	$-.0054$ (.034)
β_{23}	$-.0029$ (.313)	$-.0022$ (.450)
β_{24}	$-.0046$ (.113)	$-.0006$ (.721)
β_{34}	.0153 (.000)	.0157 (.000)
β_{1t}	$-.0008$ (.000)	$-.0008$ (.000)
β_{2t}	.0019 (.000)	.0019 (.000)
β_{3t}	.0003 (.001)	.0003 (.000)
β_{4t}	$-.0017$ (.000)	$-.0018$ (.000)
$\text{Log}L$	483.492	482.359
Positivity violations	0	0
Monotonicity violations	0	0
Curvature violations	27	0
R_1^2	.66	.64
R_2^2	.96	.50
R_3^2	.52	.98
R_4^2	.98	.96

Note: Sample period, annual data 1980-2006 ($T = 27$).

Let us consider the Morishima elasticity of substitution between oil (o) and natural gas (g), σ_{og}^m, which represents the percentage change in the o/g ratio when the relative price p_g/p_o is changed by changing p_g and holding p_o constant. As can be seen in Tables 4.22-4.24, σ_{og}^m and σ_{go}^m are both positive throughout the international sample, suggesting that oil and natural gas are consistently Morishima substitutes, irrespective of whether the price of oil or the price of natural gas changes. Similarly, oil and

Table 4.6   NQ Parameter Estimates for U.S.

Inputs:

1 = oil
2 = natural gas
3 = coal
4 = electricity

Parameter	Unrestricted	Global curvature imposed
β_1	.4582 (.000)	.4540 (.000)
β_2	.3554 (.000)	.3628 (.000)
β_3	.1710 (.000)	.1672 (.000)
β_4	.0173 (.000)	.0173 (.000)
β_{12}	−.0095 (.021)	.0007 (.722)
β_{13}	.0081 (.013)	.0037 (.242)
β_{14}	−.0004 (.848)	.0013 (.393)
β_{23}	−.0141 (.000)	−.0014 (.279)
β_{24}	−.0003 (.938)	.0015 (.413)
β_{34}	.0024 (.259)	.0100 (.002)
β_{1t}	−.0025 (.000)	−.0023 (.000)
β_{2t}	.0041 (.000)	.0037 (.000)
β_{3t}	−.0019 (.391)	−.0017 (.000)
β_{4t}	−.0005 (.000)	−.0005 (.000)
$\mathrm{Log}L$	479.170	469.575
Positivity violations	0	0
Monotonicity violations	0	0
Curvature violations	27	0
R_1^2	.80	.71
R_2^2	.97	.91
R_3^2	.91	.87
R_4^2	.88	.93

Note: Sample period, annual data 1980-2006 ($T = 27$).

coal are Morishima substitutes (irrespective of whether the price of oil or the price of coal changes), except for Italy, the United Kingdom, Hungary, China, and India.   Oil and electricity are Morishima substitutes, except for Canada, France, Japan, and Poland.   Natural gas and coal are Morishima substitutes for all countries, except for France, Japan, and South Africa; natural gas and electricity are Morishima substitutes, except for the United States, Hungary, and South Africa.   Finally, coal and electric-

Table 4.7   NQ Parameter Estimates for Poland

Inputs:

1 = oil
2 = natural gas
3 = coal
4 = electricity

Parameter	Unrestricted	Global curvature imposed
β_1	.2718 (.000)	.2668 (.000)
β_2	.3419 (.000)	.3529 (.000)
β_3	.1862 (.000)	.1875 (.000)
β_4	.1648 (.000)	.1535 (.000)
β_{12}	−.0227 (.008)	−.0091 (.117)
β_{13}	.0419 (.000)	.0413 (.000)
β_{14}	.0102 (.206)	−.0008 (.833)
β_{23}	.0214 (.013)	.0122 (.210)
β_{24}	−.0376 (.000)	−.0003 (.807)
β_{34}	−.0040 (.443)	.0012 (.824)
β_{1t}	.0104 (.000)	.0106 (.000)
β_{2t}	.0005 (.087)	.0001 (.685)
β_{3t}	.0010 (.001)	.0010 (.001)
β_{4t}	−.0054 (.000)	−.0050 (.000)
Log$L$	290.957	283.120
Positivity violations	0	0
Monotonicity violations	0	0
Curvature violations	21	0
R_1^2	.92	.91
R_2^2	.42	.70
R_3^2	.69	.87
R_4^2	.90	.92

Note: Sample period, annual data 1986-2006 ($T = 21$).

ity are Morishima substitutes, except in the case of the United Kingdom, Turkey, South Africa, and Thailand.

Regarding the Morishima elasticities of substitution, we see that in the case of the high-income countries, only the United Kingdom and the United States show some mild substitutability between coal and other fuels when the price of coal is changing. There is also strong evidence of substitutability between coal and natural gas in response to changes in the price of gas

Table 4.8   NQ Parameter Estimates for Hungary

Inputs:

1 = oil
2 = natural gas
3 = coal
4 = electricity

Parameter	Unrestricted	Global curvature imposed
β_1	.5588 (.000)	.5600 (.000)
β_2	.2509 (.000)	.2445 (.000)
β_3	.1286 (.000)	.1281 (.000)
β_4	.0538 (.000)	.0580 (.000)
β_{12}	.0205 (.070)	.0297 (.003)
β_{13}	.0272 (.007)	.0367 (.000)
β_{14}	−.0171 (.000)	−.0193 (.000)
β_{23}	−.0139 (.022)	−.0171 (.002)
β_{24}	−.0019 (.801)	.0099 (.004)
β_{34}	.0184 (.000)	.0185 (.000)
β_{1t}	−.0034 (.000)	−.0032 (.000)
β_{2t}	.0036 (.000)	.0035 (.000)
β_{3t}	.0040 (.000)	.0038 (.000)
β_{4t}	−.0015 (.000)	−.0015 (.000)
$\mathrm{Log}L$	398.636	396.032
Positivity violations	0	0
Monotonicity violations	0	0
Curvature violations	27	0
R_1^2	.69	.70
R_2^2	.84	.90
R_3^2	.90	.92
R_4^2	.95	.87

Note: Sample period, annual data 1980-2006 ($T = 27$).

($\sigma_{cg}^m = .848$) in the United Kingdom.   In the case of the upper-middle to high-income countries, only Hungary shows mild substitutability between coal and other fuels, regardless of which fuel price is changing, except for oil (see Table 4.23).   Finally, in the case of the lower-middle to low-income countries, there is some mild substitution between gas and oil ($\sigma_{go}^m = .729$) as well as between coal and oil ($\sigma_{co}^m = .412$) in South Africa, when the price of oil is changing, but not otherwise.   Thailand shows the highest potential

Table 4.9   NQ Parameter Estimates for Mexico

Inputs:

1 = oil
2 = natural gas
3 = coal
4 = electricity

Parameter	Unrestricted	Global curvature imposed
β_1	.2385 (.000)	.2367 (.000)
β_2	.5961 (.000)	.5957 (.000)
β_3	.1000 (.000)	.1012 (.000)
β_4	.0300 (.000)	.0303 (.000)
β_{12}	.0076 (.066)	.0049 (.014)
β_{13}	−.0034 (.137)	−.0029 (.000)
β_{14}	.0003 (.826)	.0016 (.069)
β_{23}	.0049 (.020)	.0064 (.000)
β_{24}	.0029 (.255)	.0024 (.360)
β_{34}	.0011 (.321)	.0001 (.793)
β_{1t}	−.0015 (.000)	−.0016 (.000)
β_{2t}	.0139 (.000)	.0140 (.000)
β_{3t}	−.0015 (.000)	−.0015 (.000)
β_{4t}	−.0009 (.000)	−.0009 (.000)
Log$L$	437.159	437.136
Positivity violations	0	0
Monotonicity violations	0	0
Curvature violations	27	0
R_1^2	.76	.77
R_2^2	.97	.92
R_3^2	.92	.75
R_4^2	.75	.97

Note: Sample period, annual data 1980-2006 ($T = 27$).

of substitution, with coal being highly substitutable with any other fuel, regardless of which direction the price change comes from. This also explains the highly elastic demand for coal in Thailand, mentioned earlier. This phenomenon of an elastic demand for coal and high substitutability between coal and the other fuels in Thailand can be explained by the structure of that economy; in particular, more than 80% of coal is used in the electricity generation sector and is readily replaceable with natural gas and other fuels.

Table 4.10 NQ Parameter Estimates for Turkey

Inputs:

1 = oil
2 = electricity
3 = coal

Parameter	Unrestricted	Global curvature imposed
β_1	.6785 (.000)	.6789 (.000)
β_2	.2264 (.000)	.2269 (.000)
β_3	.1219 (.000)	.1209 (.000)
β_{12}	.0183 (.001)	.0160 (.000)
β_{13}	.0231 (.015)	.0254 (.001)
β_{23}	−.0158 (.073)	−.0098 (.000)
β_{1t}	−.0104 (.000)	−.0103 (.000)
β_{2t}	.0075 (.000)	.0076 (.000)
β_{3t}	−.0017 (.000)	−.0019 (.000)
Log$L$	282.927	282.694
Positivity violations	0	0
Monotonicity violations	0	0
Curvature violations	27	0
R_1^2	.97	.97
R_2^2	.99	.99
R_3^2	.63	.65

Note: Sample period, annual data 1980-2006 ($T = 27$).

Overall, we can see that the elasticities of substitution obtained from the individual time-series models, presented in Tables 4.19-4.24 generally have quite small absolute values, which is not surprising given their short-run nature. These findings indicate that interfuel substitution in the short run is quite limited, regardless of the country's level of development just as predicted by theory.

4.4.2 Long-Run Estimates

To obtain the long-run elasticity estimates, we estimate a number of pooled cross-country models in accordance to (4.3), with curvature imposed over the whole pooled sample in order to attain concavity in prices. In the case of the four-fuel intercountry (cross-section) models, we are presented with

Table 4.11   NQ Parameter Estimates for Venezuela

Inputs:

1 = oil
2 = electricity
3 = natural gas

Parameter	Unrestricted	Global curvature imposed
β_1	.0887 (.000)	
β_2	.5766 (.000)	
β_3	.3198 (.000)	
β_{12}	−.0005 (.650)	
β_{13}	.0021 (.068)	
β_{23}	.0383 (.000)	
β_{1t}	−.0011 (.000)	
β_{2t}	.0047 (.000)	
β_{3t}	−.0031 (.025)	
LogL	221.522	
Positivity violations	0	
Monotonicity violations	0	
Curvature violations	0	
R_1^2	.90	
R_2^2	.64	
R_3^2	.06	

Note: Sample period, annual data 1981-1999 ($T = 19$).

the choice between two alternative ways of pooling the eight countries in question. In particular, we can estimate all countries together, or divide high-income and middle- to low-income economies into two separate poolings, each consisting of four countries (France, Japan, U.K. and the U.S. versus Poland, Hungary, Mexico, and South Africa). For the three-fuel models, however, data limitations restrict our ability to experiment with different pooling patterns, so we pool all of the respective countries together subject to data availability as described above.

The obtained long-run estimates are similar to the short-run results described above, in the sense that the theoretical regularity conditions of concavity, monotonicity, and positivity are satisfied for all data points without any significant loss in terms of the log likelihood values as demonstrated in Tables 4.25-4.26. Table 4.25 shows 9 and 7 monotonicity violations for

Table 4.12 NQ Parameter Estimates for China

Inputs:		
1 = oil		
2 = electricity		
3 = coal		
Parameter	Unrestricted	Global curvature imposed
β_1	.1730 (.000)	.1757 (.000)
β_2	.0787 (.000)	.0792 (.000)
β_3	.7500 (.000)	.7465 (.000)
β_{12}	.0132 (.284)	.0070 (.514)
β_{13}	−.0511 (.075)	−.0056 (.442)
β_{23}	.0172 (.492)	.0289 (.214)
β_{1t}	.0114 (.000)	.0113 (.000)
β_{2t}	.0081 (.000)	.0081 (.000)
β_{3t}	−.0202 (.000)	−.0200 (.000)
LogL	191.251	189.986
Positivity violations	0	0
Monotonicity violations	0	0
Curvature violations	17	0
R_1^2	.88	.88
R_2^2	.98	.98
R_3^2	.94	.94

Note: Sample period, annual data 1990-2006 ($T = 17$).

the Pooling 2 and Pooling 3 models, respectively, and Table 4.26 shows 9 monotonicity violations. Detailed inquiry has shown that these violations stem only from the fact that input shares of natural gas in South African (Table 4.25) and coal in Italy (Table 4.26) were near-zero for the first decade of the sample, making it difficult for the models to produce accurate estimated values around these points.

Comparing the alternative pooling patterns for the four-fuel models presented in Table 4.25, we conclude that the 8-countries model delivers better results than separate pools for the high vs. middle to low-income countries and, therefore, use its results for calculating the respective long-run elasticities of substitution below. On the other hand, however, the results for the three-fuel (o, g, and e) model, represented only by Canada

Table 4.13   NQ Parameter Estimates for India

Inputs:

1 = oil
2 = electricity
3 = coal

Parameter	Unrestricted	Global curvature imposed
β_1	.9540 (.000)	.9683 (.000)
β_2	.0837 (.000)	.0863 (.000)
β_3	.0245 (.000)	.0259 (.000)
β_{12}	−.0202 (.000)	.0003 (.691)
β_{13}	−.0054 (.000)	−.0002 (.583)
β_{23}	.0049 (.000)	.0013 (.004)
β_{1t}	−.0120 (.000)	−.0198 (.000)
β_{2t}	.0012 (.003)	.0032 (.003)
β_{3t}	.0008 (.000)	.0011 (.000)
LogL	297.103	281.868
Positivity violations	0	0
Monotonicity violations	0	0
Curvature violations	25	0
R_1^2	.91	.91
R_2^2	.93	.95
R_3^2	.98	.96

Note: Sample period, annual data 1981-2005 ($T = 25$).

and Venezuela turned out not to be statistically significant. Consequently, the long-run estimates for these two countries are not provided.

Tables 4.27-4.35 present the long-run elasticities of the own- and cross-price elasticities, the Allen elasticities of substitution, and the Morishima elasticities of substitution. As in the case of the short-run responses, the absolute majority of the long-run elasticities are statistically significant at conventional confidence levels. The long-run own price elasticities provided in Tables 4.27-4.29 are all negative, providing further theoretical support for our estimations. Importantly, although being on average three to four times larger than the corresponding short-run responses, the absolute values of the obtained long-run elasticities are generally still less than unity. This

Table 4.14 NQ Parameter Estimates for South Africa

Inputs:

1 = oil
2 = natural gas
3 = coal
4 = electricity

Parameter	Unrestricted	Global curvature imposed
β_1	.7631 (.000)	.7613 (.000)
β_2	.1987 (.000)	.2014 (.000)
β_3	.0057 (.000)	.0052 (.000)
β_4	.0327 (.000)	.0323 (.000)
β_{12}	.0136 (.003)	.0143 (.000)
β_{13}	.0037 (.001)	.0036 (.001)
β_{14}	.0022 (.338)	.0072 (.000)
β_{23}	−.0025 (.005)	−.0020 (.000)
β_{24}	−.0130 (.000)	−.0041 (.000)
β_{34}	−.0014 (.138)	−.0010 (.005)
β_{1t}	−.0021 (.000)	−.0021 (.000)
β_{2t}	.0020 (.000)	.0019 (.000)
β_{3t}	.0000 (.093)	.0001 (.000)
β_{4t}	−.0005 (.000)	−.0005 (.000)
Log$L$	517.776	509.496
Positivity violations	0	0
Monotonicity violations	0	0
Curvature violations	26	0
R_1^2	.83	.83
R_2^2	.89	.69
R_3^2	.72	.89
R_4^2	.89	.86

Note: Sample period, annual data 1980-2005 ($T = 26$).

indicates the limited elasticity of the demands for all fuels even in the long-run. The same conclusions apply to the long-run Allen elasticities of substitution given in Tables 4.30-4.32.

For the reasons outlined above, we concentrate our analysis of the long-run interfuel substitution on the Morishima elasticities of substitution, presented in Tables 4.33-4.35. With rare exceptions, all long-run Morishima elasticities of substitution are several times higher (in absolute values) than

Table 4.15   NQ Parameter Estimates for Thailand

Inputs:

1 = oil
2 = electricity
3 = coal

Parameter	Unrestricted	Global curvature imposed
β_1	.7819 (.000)	.7803 (.000)
β_2	.2086 (.000)	.2101 (.000)
β_3	.0047 (.256)	.0042 (.206)
β_{12}	.0488 (.000)	.0501 (.000)
β_{13}	.1066 (.005)	.1033 (.005)
β_{23}	$-$.0320 (.000)	$-$.0306 (.000)
β_{1t}	$-$.0035 (.000)	$-$.0035 (.000)
β_{2t}	.0030 (.000)	.0030 (.000)
β_{3t}	$-$.0006 (.206)	$-$.0005 (.098)
LogL	333.560	333.515
Positivity violations	0	0
Monotonicity violations	0	1
Curvature violations	27	0
R_1^2	.96	.96
R_2^2	.97	.97
R_3^2	.75	.77

Note: Sample period, annual data 1980-2006 ($T = 27$).

their short-run counterparts.   As a consequence, the long-run elasticities
are replete with examples of fuels, not substitutable in the short run, show-
ing some mild-to-high ($.4 < \sigma_{ii}^m < .9$) substitutability in the long run (coal
in France, China, and Turkey). Even more, unlike in a previous case, where
only Thailand presented some evidence of coal being highly substitutable
with other fuels, there is a multitude of such results in the long-run.   In
particular, coal is highly substitutable with any other fuel (regardless of
the direction of the price change) in the case of Italy, India, and Thailand
($\sigma_{ic}^m, \sigma_{ci}^m > 1$).   Coal is also highly substitutable with oil in the case of the
United States ($\sigma_{co}^m = 1.137$), France ($\sigma_{co}^m = .981$), and Mexico ($\sigma_{co}^m = .954$)
when the price of oil is changing. South Africa exhibits high substitutabil-
ity between natural gas and other fuels ($\sigma_{ig}^m, \sigma_{gi}^m > 2.0$), regardless of which
price is changing.

Table 4.16   Short-Run Own- and Cross-Price Elasticities for High-Income Countries

Factor i	Own- and cross-price elasticities			
	η_{io}	η_{ig}	η_{ic}	η_{ie}
Canada				
o	−.038(.009)	.052(.000)	−	−.014(.000)
g	.112(.000)	−.153(.000)	−	.041(.010)
c	−	−	−	−
e	−.011(.000)	.015(.010)	−	−.004(.190)
France				
o	−.026 (.128)	−.030 (.193)	.002 (.380)	−.005 (.467)
g	.072 (.185)	−.080 (.286)	−.007 (.403)	.015 (.548)
c	.060 (.375)	−.066 (.398)	−.006 (.606)	.012 (.594)
e	−.005 (.467)	.570 (.550)	.001 (.597)	−.001 (.714)
Japan				
o	−.034 (.000)	.034 (.000)	.003 (.326)	−.004 (.294)
g	.183 (.000)	−.184 (.000)	−.020 (.278)	.021 (.351)
c	.068 (.322)	−.068 (.351)	−.007 (.592)	.008 (.466)
e	−.002 (.295)	.002 (.349)	.000 (.466)	−.000 (.605)
Italy				
o	−.029 (.000)	−	−.001 (.031)	.030 (.000)
g	−	−	−	−
c	−.285 (.023)	−	−.016 (.264)	.301 (.031)
e	.062 (.000)	−	.003 (.040)	−.065 (.000)
U.K.				
o	−.041 (.022)	.036 (.001)	−.012 (.012)	.017 (.087)
g	.091 (.000)	−.176 (.000)	.088 (.000)	−.004 (.800)
c	−.237 (.017)	.661 (.000)	−.361 (.007)	−.062 (.384)
e	.019 (.085)	−.002 (.800)	−.004 (.392)	−.013 (.134)
U.S.				
o	−.015 (.090)	.013 (.111)	.001 (.514)	.000 (.978)
g	.026 (.106)	−.029 (.162)	.007 (.475)	−.004 (.670)
c	.071 (.501)	.144 (.496)	−.343 (.238)	.127 (.589)
e	.000 (.978)	−.001 (.670)	.002 (.578)	−.001 (.730)

Note: Numbers in parentheses are p-values.

Comparing the respective long-run and short-run results, one could also notice the interesting pattern regarding the change of signs for some of the interfuel elasticities. In particular, Tables 4.33-4.35 demonstrate that coal and electricity are complements in the long-run and substitutes in the short

Table 4.17　Short-Run Own- and Cross-Price Elasticities for Upper-Middle to High-Income Countries

Factor i	Own- and cross-price elasticities			
	η_{io}	η_{ig}	η_{ic}	η_{ie}
Poland				
o	−.064 (.000)	.094 (.000)	.001 (.933)	−.031 (.069)
g	.138 (.000)	−.238 (.000)	.010 (.786)	.090 (.046)
c	.002 (.933)	.013 (.786)	−.006 (.743)	−.010 (.592)
e	−.016 (.072)	.031 (.043)	−.003 (.591)	−.012 (.247)
Hungary				
o	−.067 (.003)	.052 (.000)	−.035 (.000)	.050 (.001)
g	.176 (.000)	−.187 (.000)	.118 (.000)	−.107 (.000)
c	−.591 (.000)	.592 (.000)	−.376 (.000)	.375 (.000)
e	.105 (.001)	−.068 (.000)	.047 (.001)	−..084 (.005)
Mexico				
o	−.014 (.495)	−.011 (.305)	.001 (.626)	.025 (.090)
g	−.026 (.299)	−.067 (.019)	.007 (.060)	.086 (.001)
c	.031 (.639)	.112 (.097)	−.138 (.039)	−.006 (.956)
e	.021 (.101)	.032 (.004)	−.000 (.956)	−.052 (.000)
Turkey				
o	−.071 (.000)	–	.035 (.000)	.036 (.000)
g	–	–	–	–
c	.246 (.000)	–	−.121 (.000)	−.125 (.000)
e	.043 (.000)	–	−.021 (.000)	−.022 (.004)
Venezuela				
o	−.043 (.000)	−.001 (.911)	–	.044 (.000)
g	−.002 (.911)	−.065 (.000)	–	.066 (.009)
c	–	–	–	–
e	.012 (.000)	.010 (.010)	–	−.022 (.001)

Note: Numbers in parentheses are p-values.

run and vise versa for all the other fuels (for example, natural gas and electricity are complements in the short run but substitutes in the long run for a number of countries). While the phenomenon of some inputs being complements in the short term and substitutes in the long term is well documented — see, for example, Griffin and Gregory (1976) — the persistent pattern of these changes is quite notable. This effect may be partly explained by the fact that most of the coal is used in the electricity generation (for example, 90% in the United States and 70% in China), hence the strong complementarity relationship.

Table 4.18   Short-Run Own- and Cross-Price Elasticities for Lower-Middle to Low-Income Countries

Factor i	\multicolumn{4}{c}{Own- and cross-price elasticities}
	η_{io}	η_{ig}	η_{ic}	η_{ie}
China				
o	−.005 (.710)	−	−.019 (.448)	.024 (.523)
g	−	−	−	−
c	−.010 (.448)	−	−.039 (.289)	.049 (.215)
e	.046 (.525)	−	.183 (.218)	−.229 (.205)
India				
o	−.004 (.433)	−	−.004 (.037)	.008 (.226)
g	−	−	−	−
c	−.032 (.042)	−	−.040 (.032)	.072 (.006)
e	.010 (.218)	−	.011 (.004)	−.020 (.034)
S. Africa				
o	−.048 (.000)	.010 (.000)	.012 (.001)	.025 (.000)
g	.676 (.000)	−.138 (.012)	−.181 (.003)	−.357 (.000)
c	.360 (.000)	−.074 (.004)	−.096 (.039)	−.190 (.000)
e	.063 (.000)	−.013 (.000)	−.017 (.000)	−.034 (.006)
Thailand				
o	−.139 (.000)	−	.054 (.000)	.085 (.000)
g	−	−	−	−
c	2.649 (.003)	−	−1.120 (.015)	−1.559 (.000)
e	.188 (.000)	−	−.068 (.000)	−.119 (.000)

Note: Numbers in parentheses are p-values.

Interfuel Substitution

Table 4.19 Short-Run Allen Elasticities of Substitution for High-Income Countries

Factor i	Allen elasticities of substitution			
	σ_{io}^a	σ_{ig}^a	σ_{ic}^a	σ_{ie}^a
Canada				
o	−.103 (.009)	.303 (.000)	—	−.030 (.000)
g		−.892 (.000)	—	.090 (.010)
c			—	—
e				−.009 (.190)
France				
o	−.065 (.130)	.178 (.187)	.149 (.375)	−.012 (.468)
g		−.493 (.281)	−.410 (.398)	.035 (.548)
c			−.352 (.605)	.028 (.595)
e				−.003 (.714)
Japan				
o	−.120 (.000)	.634 (.000)	.236 (.323)	−.006 (.294)
g		−3.350 (.000)	−1.250 (.276)	.034 (.351)
c			−.468 (.590)	.012 (.466)
e				−.000 (.605)
Italy				
o	−.043 (.000)	—	−.426 (.023)	.092 (.000)
g		—	—	—
c			−4.220 (.252)	.917 (.031)
e				−.199 (.000)
U.K.				
o	−.097 (.023)	.217 (.000)	−.561 (.017)	.045 (.086)
g		−1.053 (.000)	3.954 (.000)	−.012 (.800)
c			−16.080 (.009)	−.162 (.384)
e				−035 (.133)
U.S.				
o	−.042 (.091)	.073 (.107)	.199 (.501)	.000 (.978)
g		−.163 (.158)	.803 (.496)	−.010 (.670)
c			−38.510 (.282)	.280 (.589)
e				−.002 (.730)

Note: Numbers in parentheses are p-values.

Table 4.20   Short-Run Allen Elasticities of Substitution for Upper-Middle to High-Income Countries

Factor i	Allen elasticities of substitution			
	σ_{io}^a	σ_{ig}^a	σ_{ic}^a	σ_{ie}^a
Poland				
o	-.270 (.000)	.579 (.000)	.010 (.933)	-.067 (.071)
g		-1.457 (.000)	.080 (.786)	.192 (.046)
c			-.049 (.742)	-.019 (.591)
e				-.027 (.247)
Hungary				
o	-.123 (.002)	.325 (.000)	-1.086 (.000)	.193 (.001)
g		-1.153 (.000)	3.641 (.000)	-.418 (.000)
c			-11.610 (.000)	1.466 (.000)
e				-.330 (.006)
Mexico				
o	-.038 (.491)	-.068 (.300)	.084 (.638)	.056 (.092)
g		-.420 (.014)	.703 (.099)	.197 (.001)
c			-12.920 (.048)	-.014 (.956)
e				-.121 (.000)
Turkey				
o	-.140 (.000)	—	.486 (.000)	.086 (.000)
g		—	—	—
c			-1.689 (.028)	-.298 (.000)
e				-.052 (.004)
Venezuela				
o	-.219 (.000)	-.008 (.911)	—	.062 (.000)
g		-.634 (.000)	—	.095 (.009)
c			—	—
e				-.031 (.001)

Note: Numbers in parentheses are *p*-values.

Table 4.21   Short-Run Allen Elasticities of Substitution for Lower-Middle to Low-Income Countries

Factor i	Allen elasticities of substitution			
	σ_{io}^a	σ_{ig}^a	σ_{ic}^a	σ_{ie}^a
China				
o	-.016 (.709)	—	-.033 (.448)	.157 (.525)
g		—	—	—
c			-.070 (.288)	.327 (.218)
e				-1.536 (.209)
India				
o	-.007 (.434)	—	-.063 (.044)	.018 (.220)
g		—	—	—
c			-.620 (.036)	.170 (.006)
e				-.047 (.030)
S. Africa				
o	-.070 (.000)	.980 (.000)	.522 (.000)	.093 (.000)
g		-13.790 (.004)	-7.348 (.001)	-1.302 (.000)
c			-3.920 (.029)	-.694 (.000)
e				-.123 (.005)
Thailand				
o	-.204 (.000)	—	3.902 (.002)	.276 (.000)
g		—	—	—
c			-81.420 (.118)	-4.976 (.001)
e				-.388 (.000)

Note: Numbers in parentheses are p-values.

Table 4.22   Short-Run Morishima Elasticities of Substitution for High-
-Income Countries

| Factor i | Morishima elasticities of substitution | | | |
	σ_{io}^m	σ_{ig}^m	σ_{ic}^m	σ_{ie}^m
Canada				
o		.220 (.000)	—	−.010 (.010)
g	.152 (.000)		—	.046 (.005)
c	—	—		—
e	.029 (.000)	.184 (.000)	—	
France				
o		.111 (.000)	.008 (.002)	−.004 (.568)
g	.098 (.069)		−.001 (.922)	.015 (.517)
c	.087 (.200)	.015 (.842)		.013 (.560)
e	.021 (.002)	.087 (.000)	.006 (.000)	
Japan				
o		.222 (.000)	.011 (.003)	−.004 (.369)
g	.218 (.000)		−.012 (.501)	.022 (.338)
c	.103 (.133)	.118 (.061)		.008 (.434)
e	.033 (.000)	.188 (.000)	.007 (.000)	
Italy				
o		—	.017 (.000)	.103 (.000)
g	—		—	—
c	−.248 (.047)	—		.347 (.007)
e	.098 (.000)	—	.023 (.000)	
U.K.				
o		.223 (.000)	.366 (.000)	.031 (.002)
g	.136 (.000)		.468 (.000)	.009 (.619)
c	−.192 (.053)	.848 (.000)		−.049 (.495)
e	.063 (.000)	.185 (.000)	.375 (.000)	
U.S.				
o		.044 (.000)	.361 (.000)	.001 (.781)
g	.042 (.009)		.366 (.000)	−.003 (.767)
c	.087 (.408)	.175 (.409)		.128 (.586)
e	.016 (.000)	.029 (.000)	.362 (.000)	

Note: Numbers in parentheses are *p*-values.

Table 4.23 Short-Run Morishima Elasticities of Substitution for Upper-Middle to High-Income Countries

Factor i	Morishima elasticities of substitution			
	σ_{io}^m	σ_{ig}^m	σ_{ic}^m	σ_{ie}^m
Poland				
o		.370 (.000)	.009 (.561)	−.014 (.417)
g	.216 (.000)		.018 (.629)	.107 (.017)
c	.081 (.007)	.289 (.000)		.008 (.636)
e	.062 (.000)	.307 (.000)	.005 (.250)	
Hungary				
o		.282 (.000)	.460 (.000)	.153 (.000)
g	.280 (.000)		.613 (.000)	−.003 (.908)
c	−.489 (.000)	.821 (.000)		.480 (.000)
e	.207 (.000)	.161 (.000)	.543 (.000)	
Mexico				
o		.097 (.000)	.186 (.000)	.081 (.000)
g	.008 (.758)		.192 (.000)	.142 (.000)
c	.065 (.331)	.220 (.000)		.050 (.644)
e	.055 (.000)	.139 (.000)	.185 (.000)	
Turkey				
o		—	.160 (.000)	.057 (.000)
g	—		—	—
c	.330 (.000)	—		−.104 (.000)
e	.127 (.000)	—	.104 (.000)	
Venezuela				
o		.074 (.000)	—	.084 (.000)
g	.049 (.000)		—	.106 (.000)
c	—	—		—
e	.063 (.000)	.084 (.000)	—	

Note: Numbers in parentheses are p-values.

Table 4.24 Short-Run Morishima Elasticities of Substitution for Lower-Middle to Low-Income Countries

Factor i	σ_{io}^m	σ_{ig}^m	σ_{ic}^m	σ_{ie}^m
China				
o		—	.021 (.398)	.254 (.000)
g	—		—	—
c	−.005 (.702)	—		.280 (.000)
e	.050 (.482)	—	.223 (.134)	
India				
o		—	.038 (.000)	.036 (.000)
g	—		—	—
c	−.029 (.070)	—		.101 (.000)
e	.013 (.089)	—	.053 (.000)	
S. Africa				
o		.152 (.000)	.112 (.000)	.059 (.000)
g	.729 (.000)		−.081 (.202)	−.323 (.000)
c	.412 (.000)	.069 (.035)		−.156 (.000)
e	.116 (.000)	.129 (.000)	.082 (.000)	
Thailand				
o		—	1.206 (.000)	.204 (.000)
g	—		—	—
c	2.803 (.002)	—		−1.410 (.001)
e	.341 (.000)	—	1.084 (.000)	

Note: Numbers in parentheses are p-values.

Table 4.25   NQ Parameter Estimates for the Four-Fuel Panel Models With
Global Curvature Imposed

Inputs:

1 = oil
2 = natural gas
3 = coal
4 = electricity

Parameter	Pooling #1	Pooling #2	Pooling #3
β_1^M	.469 (.000)	.462 (.000)	.460 (.000)
β_2^M	.129 (.000)	.101 (.011)	.112 (.078)
β_3^M	.380 (.000)	.352 (.000)	.371 (.000)
β_4^M	.029 (.000)	.066 (.000)	.050 (.000)
β_{12}	.023 (.000)	−.009 (.038)	−.007 (.042)
β_{13}	−.007 (.000)	.042 (.000)	.034 (.000)
β_{14}	−.004 (.000)	.015 (.000)	.014 (.000)
β_{23}	.013 (.000)	.010 (.000)	.010 (.000)
β_{24}	.007 (.000)	.007 (.000)	.006 (.000)
β_{34}	−.002 (.000)	−.014 (.000)	−.014 (.000)
β_{1t}	−.003 (.000)	−.000 (.942)	−.002 (.000)
β_{2t}	.000 (.005)	.001 (.000)	.000 (.000)
β_{3t}	.003 (.000)	.004 (.000)	.003 (.000)
β_{4t}	−.000 (.000)	−.002 (.000)	−.002 (.000)
T	108	101	209
Log$L$	1526.25	1045.68	2290.13
Positivity violations	0	0	0
Monotonicity violations	0	9	7
Curvature violations	0	0	0
R_1^2	.81	.97	.95
R_2^2	.95	.95	.94
R_3^2	.95	.99	.98
R_4^2	.76	.90	.86

Notes: Sample period, annual data 1980-2006. M denotes mean values
of the individual country intercepts. Pooling # 1: France, Japan, U.K.,
and U.S. Pooling # 2: Poland, Hungary, Mexico, and South Africa.
Pooling # 3: All of the countries (under Pooling #1 and Pooling #2).

Table 4.26   NQ Parameter Estimates for the Three-Fuel Panel Models with Global Curvature Imposed

Inputs:	
1 = oil	
2 = coal	
3 = electricity	

Parameter	Estimates
β_1^M	.665 (.000)
β_2^M	.179 (.000)
β_3^M	.170 (.119)
β_{12}	−.012 (.009)
β_{13}	.086 (.000)
β_{23}	.014 (.019)
β_{1t}	−.007 (.000)
β_{2t}	.006 (.000)
β_{3t}	−.003 (.000)
T	123
$\mathrm{Log}L$	810.823
Positivity violations	0
Monotonicity violations	9
Curvature violations	0
R_1^2	.88
R_2^2	.98
R_3^2	.95

Notes: Sample period, annual data 1980-2006. M denotes mean values of the individual country intercepts.
Countries: Italy, Turkey, Thailand, China, and India.

Table 4.27   Long-Run Own- and Cross-Price lasticities for High-Income Countries

Factor i	Own- and cross-price elasticities			
	η_{io}	η_{ig}	η_{ic}	η_{ie}
France				
o	−.099 (.000)	−.019 (.037)	.037 (.000)	.080 (.000)
g	−.047 (.037)	−.072 (.000)	.049 (.000)	.070 (.000)
c	.882 (.000)	.467 (.000)	−.482 (.000)	−.868 (.000)
e	.077 (.000)	.027 (.000)	−.035 (.000)	−.069 (.000)
Japan				
o	−.103 (.000)	−.021 (.006)	.031 (.000)	.093 (.000)
g	−.110 (.007)	−.126 (.000)	.078 (.000)	.158 (.000)
c	.560 (.000)	.265 (.000)	−.235 (.000)	−.590 (.000)
e	.042 (.000)	.014 (.000)	−.015 (.000)	−.041 (.000)
Italy				
o	−.057 (.000)	−	.053 (.000)	.004 (.262)
g	−	−	−	−
c	3.780 (.031)	−	−3.492 (.031)	−.287 (.296)
e	.008 (.261)	−	−.008 (.225)	−.000 (.554)
U.K.				
o	−.093 (.000)	−.018 (.022)	.030 (.000)	.082 (.000)
g	−.046 (.022)	−.063 (.000)	.038 (.000)	.070 (.000)
c	.546 (.000)	.279 (.000)	−.250 (.000)	−.574 (.000)
e	.088 (.000)	.030 (.000)	−.034 (.000)	−.085 (.000)
U.S.				
o	−.093 (.000)	−.021 (.051)	.029 (.000)	.085 (.000)
g	−.042 (.051)	−.082 (.000)	.040 (.000)	.084 (.000)
c	1.044 (.000)	.715 (.000)	−.502 (.000)	−1.257 (.000)
e	.066 (.000)	.033 (.000)	−.027 (.000)	−.072 (.000)

Note: Numbers in parentheses are p-values.

Table 4.28   Long-Run Own- and Cross-Price Elasticities for Upper-Middle to High-Income Countries

Factor i	Own- and cross-price elasticities			
	η_{io}	η_{ig}	η_{ic}	η_{ie}
Poland				
o	−.118 (.000)	−.042 (.000)	.053 (.000)	.106 (.000)
g	−.062 (.000)	−.062 (.000)	.052 (.000)	.071 (.000)
c	.100 (.000)	.067 (.000)	−.065 (.000)	−.103 (.000)
e	.055 (.000)	.025 (.000)	−.028 (.000)	−.051 (.000)
Hungary				
o	−.081 (.000)	−.010 (.054)	.033 (.000)	.058 (.000)
g	−.034 (.054)	−.040 (.000)	.037 (.000)	.038 (.000)
c	.558 (.000)	.184 (.000)	−.302 (.000)	−.440 (.000)
e	.125 (.000)	.024 (.000)	−.056 (.000)	−.093 (.000)
Mexico				
o	−.211 (.000)	.015 (.714)	.027 (.000)	.169 (.000)
g	.036 (.714)	−.257 (.005)	.043 (.000)	.178 (.000)
c	.743 (.000)	.497 (.000)	−.199 (.000)	−1.040 (.000)
e	.137 (.000)	.062 (.000)	−.031 (.000)	−.168 (.000)
Turkey				
o	−.095 (.000)	—	.104 (.000)	−.009 (.168)
g	—	—	—	—
c	.714 (.000)	—	−.784 (.000)	.070 (.209)
e	−.011 (.168)	—	.012 (.207)	−.001 (.501)

Note: Numbers in parentheses are *p*-values.

Table 4.29   Long-Run Own- and Cross-Price Elasticities for Lower-Middle to Low-Income Countries

Factor i	Own- and cross-price elasticities			
	η_{io}	η_{ig}	η_{ic}	η_{ie}
China				
o	−.272 (.000)	−	.311 (.000)	−.039 (.014)
g	−	−	−	−
c	.161 (.000)	−	−.184 (.000)	.023 (.025)
e	−.075 (.013)	−	.086 (.025)	−.011 (.196)
India				
o	−.113 (.000)	−	.203 (.000)	−.090 (.000)
g	−	−	−	−
c	1.453 (.000)	−	−2.602 (.000)	1.149 (.001)
e	−.107 (.000)	−	.191 (.001)	−.084 (.015)
S. Africa				
o	−.069 (.000)	−.011 (.291)	.022 (.000)	.058 (.000)
g	−.716 (.365)	−2.435 (.078)	1.135 (.069)	2.016 (.071)
c	.612 (.000)	.486 (.000)	−.345 (.006)	−.752 (.000)
e	.146 (.000)	.077 (.000)	−.067 (.000)	−.156 (.000)
Thailand				
o	−.034 (.000)	−	.033 (.000)	.002 (.643)
g	−	−	−	−
c	1.676 (.002)	−	−1.598 (.002)	−.078 (.628)
e	.004 (.643)	−	−.003 (.627)	−.000 (.811)

Note: Numbers in parentheses are p-values.

Table 4.30   Long-Run Allen Elasticities of Substitution for High-Income Countries

Factor i	Allen elasticities of substitution			
	σ_{io}^a	σ_{ig}^a	σ_{ic}^a	σ_{ie}^a
France				
o	-.247 (.000)	-.118 (.037)	2.202 (.000)	.191 (.000)
g		-.445 (.000)	2.889 (.000)	.166 (.000)
c			-28.345 (.001)	-2.063 (.000)
e				-.163 (.000)
Japan				
o	-.357 (.000)	-.381 (.007)	1.934 (.000)	.146 (.000)
g		-2.280 (.000)	4.799 (.000)	.248 (.000)
c			-14.464 (.000)	-.924 (.000)
e				-.064 (.000)
Italy				
o	-.086 (.000)	—	5.702 (.029)	.130 (.262)
g		—	—	—
c			-377.581 (.277)	-.876 (.296)
e				-.002 (.553)
U.K.				
o	-.221 (.000)	-.109 (.022)	1.295 (.000)	.210 (.000)
g		-.374 (.000)	1.672 (.000)	.181 (.000)
e			-1.478 (.000)	-1.477 (.000)
c				$-.218$ (.000)
U.S.				
o	-.261 (.000)	-.118 (.051)	2.938 (.000)	.186 (.000)
g		-.456 (.000)	3.999 (.000)	.184 (.000)
c			-50.730 (.005)	-2.757 (.000)
e				-.158 (.000)

Note: Numbers in parentheses are p-values.

Table 4.31   Long-Run Allen Elasticities of Substitution for Upper-Middle to High-Income Countries

Factor i	Allen elasticities of substitution			
	σ_{io}^a	σ_{ig}^a	σ_{ic}^a	σ_{ie}^a
Poland				
o	-.490 (.000)	-.257 (.000)	.418 (.000)	.227 (.000)
g		-.377 (.000)	.411 (.000)	.151 (.000)
c			-.508 (.000)	-.219 (.000)
e				-.109 (.000)
Hungary				
o	-.148 (.000)	-.063 (.054)	1.016 (.000)	.228 (.000)
g		-.249 (.000)	1.136 (.000)	.147 (.000)
c			-9.204 (.000)	-1.724 (.000)
e				-.362 (.000)
Mexico				
o	-.569 (.000)	.097 (.714)	1.999 (.000)	.370 (.000)
g		-1.622 (.006)	3.140 (.000)	.389 (.000)
c			-14.568 (.000)	-2.279 (.000)
e				-.367 (.000)
Turkey				
o	-.188 (.000)	—	1.410 (.000)	-.022 (.168)
g		—	—	—
c			-10.584 (.000)	.167 (.209)
e				-.003 (.501)

Note: Numbers in parentheses are p-values.

Table 4.32   Long-Run Allen Elasticities of Substitution for Lower-Middle to Low-Income Countries

Factor i	σ^a_{io}	σ^a_{ig}	σ^a_{ic}	σ^a_{ie}
		Allen elasticities of substitution		
China				
o	-.939 (.000)	—	.554 (.000)	-.259 (.014)
g		—	—	—
c			-.327 (.000)	.153 (.025)
e				-.071 (.197)
India				
o	-.225 (.000)	—	2.879 (.000)	-.211 (.000)
g		—	—	—
c			-36.876 (.010)	2.704 (.001)
e				-.198 (.017)
S. Africa				
o	-.099 (.000)	-1.037 (.363)	.885 (.000)	.211 (.000)
g		-233.107 (.341)	46.503 (.066)	7.358 (.068)
c			-14.138 (.000)	-2.746 (.000)
e				-.568 (.000)
Thailand				
o	-.051 (.000)	—	2.462 (.001)	.005 (.643)
g		—	—	—
c			-119.855 (.079)	-254 (.628)
e				-.000 (.811)

Note: Numbers in parentheses are p-values.

Interfuel Substitution

Table 4.33 Long-Run Morishima Elasticities of Substitution for High-
-Income Countries

Factor i	Morishima elasticities of substitution			
	σ_{io}^m	σ_{ig}^m	σ_{ic}^m	σ_{ie}^m
France				
o		.053 (.000)	.519 (.000)	.149 (.000)
g	.052 (.023)		.531 (.000)	.139 (.000)
c	.981 (.000)	.539 (.000)		−.799 (.000)
e	.176 (.000)	.099 (.000)	.447 (.000)	
Japan				
o		.105 (.000)	.266 (.000)	.134 (.000)
g	−.007 (.866)		.312 (.000)	.199 (.000)
c	.663 (.000)	.391 (.000)		−.549 (.000)
e	.146 (.000)	.140 (.000)	.220 (.000)	
Italy				
o		−	3.545 (.031)	.005 (.196)
g	−		−	−
c	3.837 (.028)	−		−.287 (.297)
e	.066 (.000)	−	3.484 (.035)	
U.K.				
o		.044 (.000)	.280 (.000)	.166 (.000)
g	.047 (.020)		.289 (.000)	.155 (.000)
c	.639 (.000)	.342 (.000)		−.490 (.000)
e	.181 (.000)	.093 (.000)	.216 (.000)	
U.S.				
o		.060 (.000)	.531 (.000)	.157 (.000)
g	.051 (.019)		.542 (.000)	.156 (.000)
c	1.137 (.000)	.797 (.000)		−1.185 (.000)
e	.159 (.000)	.114 (.000)	.475 (.000)	

Note: Numbers in parentheses are *p*-values.

Table 4.34   Long-Run Morishima Elasticities of Substitution for Upper-Middle to High-Income Countries

Factor i	Morishima elasticities of substitution			
	σ_{io}^{m}	σ_{ig}^{m}	σ_{ic}^{m}	σ_{ie}^{m}
Poland				
o		.020 (.025)	.118 (.000)	.158 (.000)
g	.056 (.000)		.117 (.000)	.122 (.000)
c	.218 (.000)	.129 (.000)		−.051 (.000)
e	.172 (.000)	.086 (.000)	.037 (.000)	
Hungary				
o		.030 (.000)	.335 (.000)	.151 (.000)
g	.047 (.009)		.339 (.000)	.130 (.000)
c	.640 (.000)	.224 (.000)		−.348 (.000)
e	.207 (.000)	.064 (.000)	.246 (.000)	
Mexico				
o		.272 (.000)	.227 (.000)	.336 (.000)
g	.247 (.012)		.242 (.000)	.345 (.000)
c	.954 (.000)	.753 (.000)		−.873 (.000)
e	.349 (.000)	.318 (.000)	.168 (.000)	
Turkey				
o		−	.888 (.000)	−.008 (.224)
g	−		−	−
c	.809 (.000)	−		.071 (.202)
e	.084 (.000)	−	.796 (.000)	

Note: Numbers in parentheses are *p*-values.

Table 4.35　Long-Run Morishima Elasticities of Substitution for Lower-Middle to Low-Income Countries

Factor i	σ_{io}^m	σ_{ig}^m	σ_{ic}^m	σ_{ie}^m
China				
o		—	.494 (.000)	−.028 (.074)
g	—		—	—
c	.433 (.000)	—		.033 (.001)
e	.197 (.000)	—	.269 (.000)	
India				
o		—	2.805 (.000)	−.005 (.773)
g	—		—	—
c	1.566 (.000)	—		1.233 (.000)
e	.007 (.760)	—	2.792 (.000)	
S. Africa				
o		2.424 (.053)	.367 (.000)	.214 (.000)
g	−.648 (.412)		1.480 (.017)	2.172 (.051)
c	.680 (.000)	2.921 (.020)		−.597 (.000)
e	.214 (.000)	2.512 (.045)	.278 (.000)	
Thailand				
o		—	1.631 (.000)	.002 (.609)
g	—		—	—
c	1.710 (.001)	—		−.078 (.629)
e	.038 (.000)	—	1.595 (.000)	

Note: Numbers in parentheses are p-values.

4.5   Concluding Comment

We have investigated interfuel substitution both in the short- and long-run contexts, taking a flexible functional form approach and using state-of-the-art recent advances in microeconometrics. Several important conclusions can be drawn from our results. First of all, the obtained long-run interfuel elasticities of substitution are generally significantly higher than their short-run counterparts. Secondly, there seems to be convincing evidence of coal being a consistent mild-to-high complement for electricity and a substitute for other fuels on a national level in the long run. However, for other fuels such as oil, natural gas, and electricity, our evidence indicates that the interfuel elasticities of substitution are in general consistently below unity, revealing the limited ability (mild at best) to substitute one source of energy for another and suggesting that fossil fuels will continue to maintain their major role as a source of energy in the near future.

Finally, our results do not suggest any significant differences between the three groups of countries in terms of interfuel substitution at the national level either in the short-run or in the long-run context. That is, interfuel substitution seems to depend on the structure of the economy and the horizon of adjustment, but to be independent of the level of economic development. Also, because interfuel substitution is limited in the near term, there will be a greater need for relative price changes to induce switching to a lower carbon economy.

Bibliography

Attfield, C.L.F. "Estimating a Cointegrating Demand System." *European Economic Review* 41 (1997), 61-73.

Baltagi, B.H. *Econometric Analysis of Panel Data*. New York: John Wiley and Sons (1995).

Baltagi, B.H. and J.M. Griffin. "Pooled Estimators vs. their Heterogeneous Counterparts in the Context of Dynamic Demand for Gasoline." *Journal of Econometrics* 77 (1997), 303-327.

Barnett, W.A. "Tastes and Technology: Curvature is not Sufficient for Regularity." *Journal of Econometrics* 108 (2002), 199-202.

Barnett, W.A. and M. Pasupathy. "Regularity of the Generalized Quadratic Production Model: A Counterexample." *Econometric Reviews* 22 (2003), 135-154.

Barnett, W.A. and A. Serletis. "Consumer Preferences and Demand Systems." *Journal of Econometrics* 147 (2008), 210-224.

Barnett, W.A. and P. Yue. "Semi-nonparametric Estimation of the Asymptotically Ideal Model: The AIM Demand System." In G. Rhodes and T.B. Fomby (Eds.), *Advances in Econometrics*, Vol VII. Greenwich, CT: JAI Press (1988).

Barnett, W.A., J. Geweke, and M. Wolfe. "Semi-Nonparametric Bayesian Estimation of the Asymptotically Ideal Production Model." *Journal of Econometrics* 49 (1991), 5-50.

Barten, A.P. "Maximum Likelihood Estimation of a Complete System of Demand Equations." *European Economic Review* 1 (1969), 7-73.

Berndt, E.R. and L.R. Christensen. "The Internal Structure of Functional Relationships: Separability, Substitution and Aggregation." *Review of Economic Studies* 60 (1973), 403-410.

Berndt, E.R. and N.E. Savin. "Estimation and Hypothesis Testing in Singular Equation Systems with Autoregressive Disturbances." *Econometrica* 43 (1975), 937-957.

Berndt, E.R. and D. Wood. "Technology, Prices, and the Derived Demand for Energy." *Review of Economics and Statistics* 57 (1975), 259-268.

Blackorby, C. and R.R. Russell. "Will the Real Elasticity of Substitution Please Stand Up?" *American Economic Review* 79 (1989), 882-888.

Burnside, C. "Production Function Regressions, Returns to Scale, and Externalities." *Journal of Monetary Economics* 37 (1996), 177–201.

Caves, D. and L.R. Christensen. "Global Properties of Flexible Functional Forms." *American Economic Review* 70 (1980), 422-432.

Christensen, L., D.W. Jorgenson, and L.J. Lau. "Transendendal Logarithmic Utility Functions." *American Economic Review* 65 (1975), 367-364.

Cobb, C.W. and P.H. Douglas. "A Theory of Production." *American Economic Review* 18 (1928), 139-165.

Considine, T.J. "Separability, Functional Form, and Regulatory Policy in Models of Interfuel Substitution." *Energy Economics* 11 (1989), 82-94.

Diewert, W.E. "An Application of the Shephard Duality Theorem: A Generalized Leontief Production Function." *Journal of Political Economy* 79 (1971), 481-507.

Diewert, W.E. "Functional Forms for Profit and Transformation Functions." *Journal of Economic Theory* 6 (1973), 284-316.

Diewert, W.E. "Applications of Duality Theory." In M.D. Intriligator and D.A. Kendrick, eds., *Frontiers of Quantitative Economics*, Vol. II, Amsterdam: North-Holland (1974), pp. 106-171.

Diewert, W.E. and K.J. Fox. "On the Estimation of Returns to Scale, Technical Progress and Monopolistic Markups." *Journal of Econometrics* 145 (2008), 174-193.

Diewert, W.E. and K.J. Fox. "The Normalized Quadratic Expenditure Function." In *Quantifying Consumer Preferences*, Ed.: D.J. Slottje. Emerald (2009), pp. 149-178.

Diewert, W.E. and T.J. Wales. "Flexible Functional Forms and Global Curvature Conditions." *Econometrica* 55 (1987), 43-68.

Diewert, W.E. and T.J. Wales. "Normalized Quadratic Systems of Consumer Demand Functions." *Journal of Business and Economic Statistics* 6 (1988), 303-312.

Diewert, W.E. and T.J. Wales. "Quadratic Spline Models for Producer's Supply and Demand Functions." *International Economic Review* 33 (1992), 705-722.

Denny, M. and M. Fuss. "The Use of Approximation Analysis to Test for Separability and the Existence of Consistent Aggregates." *American Economic Review* 67 (1977), 404-418.

Feng, G. and A. Serletis. "Productivity Trends in U.S. Manufacturing: Evidence from the NQ and AIM Cost Functions." *Journal of Econometrics* 142 (2008), 281-311.

Fuss, M.A. "The Demand for Energy in Canadian Manufacturing: An Example of the Estimation of Production Structures with Many Inputs." *Journal of Econometrics* 5 (1977), 89-116.

Gallant, A.R. "On the Bias in Flexible Functcional Forms and an Essentially Unbiased Form: The Fourier Flexible Form." *Journal of Econometrics* 15 (1981), 211-245.

Griffin, J.M. *Energy Conservation in the OECD: 1980 to 2000.* Cambridge, MA: Ballinger (1979).

Griffin, J.M. and P.R. Gregory. "An Intercountry Translog Model of Energy Substitution Responses." *American Economic Review* 66 (1976), 845-857.

Guilkey, D., C. Lovell, and R. Sickles. "A Comparison of the Performance of Three Flexible Functional Forms." *International Economic Review* 24 (1983), 591-616.

Hall, V.B. "Major OECD Country Industrial Sector Interfuel Substitution Estimates, 1960-1979." *Energy Economics* 8 (1986), 74-89.

Houthakker, H. "New Evidence on Demand Elasticities." *Econometrica* 33 (1965), 277-288.

Jones, C.T. "A Dynamic Analysis of Interfuel Substitution in U.S. Industrial Energy Demand." *Journal of Business and Economic Statistics* 13 (1995), 459-465.

Jones, C.T. "A Pooled Analysis of Interfuel Substitution in Industrial Energy Demand by the G-7 Countries." *Applied Economics* 28 (1996), 815-821.

Lau, L.J. "Testing and Imposing Monotonicity, Convexity, and Quasi-Convexity Constraints." In M. Fuss and D. McFadden (Eds.), *Production Economics: A Dual Approach to Theory and Applications* Vol. 1. Amsterdam: North Holland (1978), pp. 409-453.

Moschini, G. "Imposing Local Curvature in Flexible Demand Systems." *Journal of Business and Economic Statistics* 17 (1999), 487-490.

Ng, S. "Testing for Homogeneity in Demand Systems When the Regressors are Nonstationary." *Journal of Applied Econometrics* 10 (1995), 147-163.

Phillips, P.C.B. "Fully Modified Least Squares and Vector Autoregression." *Econometrica* 62 (1995), 1023-1078.

Pindyck, R.S. "Interfuel Substitution and the Industrial Demand for Energy: An International Comparison." *Review of Economics and Statistics* 61 (1979), 169-179.

Ryan, D.L. and T.J. Wales. "A Simple Method for Imposing Local Curvature in Some Flexible Consumer Demand Systems." *Journal of Business and Economic Statistics* 16 (1998), 331-338.

Ryan, D.L. and T.J. Wales. "Imposing Local Concavity in the Translog and Generalized Leontief Cost Functions." *Economics Letters* 67 (2000), 253-260.

Serletis, A. "Monetary Asset Separability Tests." In W.A. Barnett and K.J. Singleton (Eds.), *New Approaches to Monetary Economics*. Cambridge: Cambridge University Press (1987), pp. 169-182.

Serletis, A. and A. Shahmoradi. "Semi-nonparametric Estimates of Interfuel Substitution in U.S. Energy Demand." *Energy Economics* 30 (2008), 2123-2133.

Serletis, A., G. Timilsina, and O. Vasetsky. "Interfuel Substitution in the United States." *Energy Economics* 32 (2010), 737-745.

Serletis, A., G. Timilsina, and O. Vasetsky. "International Evidence on Sectoral Interfuel Substitution." *The Energy Journal* 31 (2010), 1-29.

Serletis, A., G. Timilsina, and O. Vasetsky. "International Evidence on Aggregate Short-Run and Long-Run Interfuel Substitution." *Energy Economics* 33 (2011), 209-216.

Shephard, R.W. *Cost and Production Functions*. Princeton: Princeton University Press (1953).

Söderholm, P. "Fuel Flexibility in the West European Power Sector." *Resources Policy* 26 (2000), 157-170.

Stock, J.H. and M.W. Watson. "A Simple Estimator of Cointegrating Vectors in Higher Order Integrated Systems." *Econometrica* 61 (1993), 783-820.

Urga, G. and C. Walters. "Dynamic Translog and Linear Logit Models: A Factor Demand Analysis of Interfuel Substitution in U.S. Industrial Energy Demand." *Energy Economics* 25 (2003), 1-21.

Uri, N.D. "Energy Consumption in the U.K., 1948-64." *Energy Economics* 1 (1979), 241-244.

Uzawa, H. "Duality Principles in the Theory of Cost and Production. *International Economic Review* 5 (1964), 216-220.

General Index

Author Index